FORAGING
SOUTHERN
CALIFORNIA

118 Nutritious, Tasty, and Abundant Foods

Douglas Kent

Adventure Publications
Cambridge, Minnesota

ın

.s dedicated to a fantastic clan of foragers: the Dunne family
Peter, Shannon, Connor, Declan, and Kieran) and the faculty,
d students at the Lyle Center for Regenerative Studies, Califor-
.te Polytechnic University, Pomona.

er and book design by Jonathan Norberg

.dited by Brett Ortler

Cover images: Prickly Pear Fruit, front cover by **Lynda Disher/shutterstock.com**; Wild
Strawberry, back cover by **Sarah2/shutterstock.com**

Photo credits:

Photos identified by page in descending positions a, b, c, d, e, f
All photos copyright of their respective photographers.
Alex Bairstow: 225c; **Ross Bayton:** 81a; **Thomas A. Benson:** 190; **Chet Blackburn:** 35c, 91c
119b; **Aaron Carlson:** 36, 215b, 221b; **d24bishop:** 120; **Douglas Kent:** 19c, 31b, 32, 43a, 81b, 83d,
96, 100 inset, 107a, 128, 180, 210, 212, 229, 230a, 230b, 236, 256; **Jim Morefield:** 71c, 77b, 82;
PUBLIC DOMAIN/Anthony Valois and the National Park Service: 35a, 91a, https://en.wiki
pedia.org/wiki/Hesperocnide_tenella#/media/File:Hesperocnidetenella.jpg; **PUBLIC
DOMAIN/JoJan:** 189, https://commons.wikimedia.org/wiki/File:Artemisia_californica01.jpg;
PUBLIC DOMAIN/KP Botany: 19b, 104, https://commons.wikimedia.org/wiki/File:Vitis_cali
fornica_with_grapes.jpg; **PUBLIC DOMAIN/PiPi69E-Own Work:** 171, https://upload.wiki
media.org/wikipedia/commons/3/38/Asarum_caudatum_1.jpg

10 9 8 7 6 5 4 3

Foraging Southern California: 118 Nutritious, Tasty and Abundant Foods
Copyright © 2020 by Douglas Kent
Published by Adventure Publications
An imprint of AdventureKEEN
310 Garfield Street South
Cambridge, Minnesota 55008
(800) 678-7006
www.adventurepublications.net
All rights reserved
Printed in China
ISBN 978-1-59193-915-3 (pbk.); ISBN 978-1-59193-916-0 (ebook)

Table of Contents

BERRIES

High in nutrients, sugars, and ridiculously easy to eat, berries are favorites of hikers, bikers and explorers. Better yet, many of the best berries ripen in summer, the peak period for beginning foragers.

The berries in this section are not only edible, but divine. Unfortunately, not all berries are heaven's gift. Some will make you seriously ill. As a rule: always compare your finds to the comparable species in this guide, other books on foraging and reputed websites, such as Calflora (www.calflora.org). In other words, stick with the berries below until you have read other books, foraged often, and feel comfortable around a large variety of fruit-bearing plants.

IMPORTANT: Always rinse and clean berries before eating.

BLACKBERRY
(Rubus spp.)

WILD

TYPE: Biennial vining shrub
STATUS: Native and non-native
LEAF ARRANGEMENT: Alternate
HARVEST TIME: Summer

WARNING: This vine or shrub has thorns along its branches.

HABITAT: Tolerant of shade, salty soil, and compacted conditions, blackberry is found as often around human development as it is in the wild. It prefers ravines, canyons, and natural woodlands, and it grows all along the coast and at elevations up to 7,400 feet in the San Bernardino Mountains. Because it requires moderate amounts of rainfall, blackberry is not well suited to life in the desert.

GROWTH: This is an aggressive tumbling plant and can create a thicket that's 5 feet tall and 20 feet wide under the right conditions. Their long vine-like, densely thorny branches are their distinguishing characteristic. The plant spreads by crown sprouting, rooting along stems, sprouting from roots, and via seeds. Stems are biennial and only live two years.

LEAVES: Thin prickly stems terminate to either a single leaf or 3–5 leaflets. The single leaf is shaped like a triangle or a fan; both are deeply lobed. The leaflets are oblong or lance-like and have a pronounced point. The leaves are 2–4.5 inches long, serrated and toothed, somewhat bristly, and arranged alternately along the stem.

FLOWERS: Growing from the ends of the stems, flowers are found in clusters of 2 to 15. The flower seems old-fashioned in its simplicity: 5 distinct petals, muted colors, and an abundance of pollen-tipped filaments at the center. Color ranges from soft white to pale pink.

BERRY: Red and hard when immature, and soft and a glistening midnight purple when ripe, the blackberry is a composite of many small berries, called drupelets. It is oblong or dome-shaped and never more than 0.75 inch long. Hair between the drupelets is common. Fruit occurs on second-year stems.

SEASON: Summer

BENEFITS: Rich in fiber, manganese, and vitamins C and K, blackberry is an antioxidant and an anti-inflammatory.

OTHER NAMES: Bramble

poison oak   poison ivy

COMPARABLE SPECIES: Poison oak and ivy grow in the same areas as blackberry (page 98). Sometimes they are found intertwined. Neither of these plants have thorns. Please refer to the chapter (page 14) on poisonous plants for details. Other thorny, sprawling plants include raspberry and trailing rose, both of which produce edible fruit.

NOTES: Eat the berries fresh or dried. They are sweet, yummy, and addictive. You can make a tea from fresh or dried leaves; it is high in antitoxins and vitamin C, although it also contains tannins.

Golden currant

CURRANT AND GOOSEBERRY
(Ribes spp.)

WILD

TYPE: Shrub; mountainous species are deciduous; coastal species are evergreen
STATUS: Native
LEAF ARRANGEMENT: Opposite, simple, and palmately lobed
HARVEST TIME: Late spring through summer

WARNING: Gooseberries have extensive thorns and spines along their branches and stems.

HABITAT: There are more than 35 different species of *Ribes* growing in Southern California. They can be found along the coast, throughout the mountains, and in the more protected areas of the desert. They can even be found on Catalina Island and at elevations of up to 10,000 feet. Look for them in cool canyons, below forests, and above streams.

GROWTH: The height and width vary greatly between species: they can be 2–12 feet tall and 1–10 feet wide; the plants are generally woody and airy. Gooseberries have thorns and spines along their branches, stems, and fruits; currants do not. Mountainous species are deciduous; coastal species are evergreen. The best way to identify *Ribes* is through their leaves.

LEAVES: While leaf size varies greatly between species, the general leaf pattern is the same: older leaves have 5 lobes (palmately lobed), and younger leaves have 3 lobes. Distinct and indented veins run down the middle of the lobes; the leaf surface texture is coarse, and the margins are lightly toothed.

FLOWERS: Dangling from wispy stems along branches, petite flowers cascade from the area near the axis of the branches and leaves. They are tiny and resemble fuchsia. The flowers have 5–6 sepals, 5 tiny petals, and 5 noticeable stamens. Colors range from coral, pink, and red to white, green, and yellow. *Ribes* blooms between January and July. The flowers are a delight but easy to miss.

BERRY: Small and shaped like a blueberry, some varieties are vigorous fruit producers, while others aren't. Berries are no larger than 0.6 inch in diameter. Berry color varies from blue and green to pink, purple, red, white, and yellow.

SEASON: Coastal berries begin to ripen in spring; mountainous varieties ripen in summer.

BENEFITS: Berries are high in iron, phosphorus, and vitamin C.

OTHER NAMES: None

poison oak

COMPARABLE SPECIES: Young *Ribes* leaves have 3 lobes and look somewhat similar to the leaves of poison oak (page 30). If all the leaf's margins are joined at the 3 lobes, it is not poison oak.

NOTES: While all *Ribes* berries are edible, not all are tasty. Many are astringent. Berries are eaten raw, dried, or cooked.

ELDERBERRY, BLACK AND BLUE
(Sambucus nigra and *S. nigra* ssp. *caerulea)*

WILD

TYPE: Evergreen or a semi-deciduous shrub or tree
STATUS: Native
LEAF ARRANGEMENT: Odd-pinnate
HARVEST TIME: Summer and fall

WARNING: Too many raw berries will cause diarrhea.

HABITAT: Elderberry is versatile; it grows in deep or shallow soils and in sun or shade, but it needs at least 12 inches of annual rainfall. It is easily found in and around coastal or mountainous canyons or ravines, including those near urban areas. Protected ravines in the desert mountains might also have this lush-looking shrub.

GROWTH: This shrub or tree can grow up to 30 feet tall and 20 feet wide. Its branches get lanky and often sag under the weight of its foliage and fruit. One of its most distinguishing characteristics is the stench of its leaves and sap; break a leaf or stem, and if you are repelled by the odor, it's elderberry. It becomes deciduous amid a severe drought or freeze.

LEAVES: Leaves are divided into 3 or 9 pairs of leaflets, and each leaflet is 1–6 inches long, oval or elliptical, lightly serrated, and features pronounced points.

FLOWERS: Clusters of creamy white, fragrant flowers the size of your hand erupt from the shrub March through July. The umbrella-like clusters (inflorescence) are a composite of many tiny stems and flowers.

BERRY: Bountiful masses of small, 0.25-inch berries cover this shrub. They are a deep, dark bluish black. The berries are often covered in a milky film, which makes them look purplish or light blue.

SEASON: Ripe berries become available from late spring through early fall. The flowering season on some plants might last 5 months: March through July and sometimes beyond.

BENEFITS: These beautiful and abundant berries, when cooked, are high in iron, and potassium, as well as vitamins A, B6, and C. They also have measurable amounts of other vital nutrients. The berries are considered anti-inflammatory. Both the berries and flowers are made into extracts and teas and used to treat colds and fevers.

OTHER NAMES: Mexican elderberry

red elderberry

COMPARABLE SPECIES: Although not naturally found in Southern California, the red elderberry looks similar. It grows in the Sierra Nevada Mountains and its red berries are poisonous unless cooked.

NOTES: Not the sweetest berry, but refreshing and easy to find. Eat raw or dry, but only in small doses; it is a laxative in large amounts. If planning to eat large quantities, cook the berries first, which destroys the diarrhea-causing chemicals. Flowers are eaten raw or cooked or made into a tea that can be used to reduce the severity of colds and fevers. **IMPORTANT:** Do not eat the leaves, stems, or green berries—all are poisonous.

GRAPE, WILD
(Vitis californica and *V. girdiana)*

WILD ORNAMENTAL

TYPE: Deciduous vine

STATUS: Native

LEAF ARRANGEMENT: Leaves, flowers, and tendrils grow from nodes

HARVEST TIME: Summer for berries; midwinter through spring for leaves

HABITAT: Wild grape is found along the coast, on both sides of the coastal mountains, and in the wetter niches of the mountainous desert. It is an understory native and likely found in canyons, ravines, and woodland environments. It cannot be found at elevations above 4,500 feet or in areas with less than 7 inches of annual rainfall. It is common in native gardens throughout the state.

GROWTH: Wild grape looks like its cultivated cousin; it has long, lanky branches that scramble 40 feet or more and have flaking, peeling bark. It climbs up trees, spills down canyons, and covers large expanses. New stems are supple and light green; old branches are hard, mud brown, and shed bark. Grape's clinging tendrils are what set it apart from other large-leafed understory plants.

LEAVES: Rounded or heart-shaped, fuzzy, and 3–5 inches across, a grape's leaf is a rich green with silvery hues. Leaf margins vary and range from lobed to smooth or toothed. Leaves turn a vivid pumpkin-orange or purplish red in fall.

FLOWERS: Clusters of creamy green, yellow, and/or white tiny flowers cascade from the ends of stems. Clusters are 2–6 inches in length and bloom May–June. Bees love them.

BERRIES: Rarely more than 0.25 inch in diameter and midnight purple or bluish black, these berries are sometimes difficult to spot in understory environments. They droop in clusters from the ends of the spindly stems.

SEASON: Fruit ripens in summer. Leaves are harvested for greens midwinter through spring; they can be used year-round as a food wrap.

BENEFITS: Leaves are rich in fiber, calcium, and vitamins C and K.

OTHER NAMES: Desert grape, Southern California grape

Algerian ivy

Abutilon

COMPARABLE SPECIES: There are two similar plants. Algerian ivy's leaves look somewhat like grape, and they are both ground covers and can be found growing together. Algerian ivy is poisonous, and its leaf is shiny with smooth margins. Species of the genus *Abutilon*, which can be native, invasive, or ornamental, also have a similar leaf and are understory plants as well. However, these plants grow upright and do not scramble. *Abutilon* leaf and green fruit should be considered inedible, although the flowers are edible.

NOTES: Berries are eaten raw, dried, or cooked, but mostly raw because they aren't often abundant. Tendrils are eaten raw. Young leaves are eaten raw or steamed.

Sugar bush

WILD

LEMONADE BERRY AND SUGAR BUSH
(Rhus integrifolia and Rhus ovata)

TYPE: Evergreen shrub
STATUS: Native
LEAF ARRANGEMENT: Opposite and oval
HARVEST TIME: Mid-spring through summer

HABITAT: Lemonade berry can be found all along the coast and at elevations of up to 2,500 feet in the coastal foothills. Sugar bush tolerates considerably more cold and can be found at elevations of 5,000 feet in the coastal mountains, on their eastern flanks, and in the wetter parts of the desert mountains. Neither is a solitary plant, and both are found in the company of many other perennials, shrubs, and trees. Both require at least 11 inches of rainfall per year.

GROWTH: Depending on the moisture levels and wind shear present, they grow 3–12 feet tall and wide. They have a short, stout trunk and many strong, flexible branches. Their shiny, leathery leaves on reddish stems are their defining characteristic.

LEAVES: The shiny, tough leaves are oval or rounded and 1–3 inches long. Lemonade berry leaves have smooth or wavy margins; older leaves may have tiny spines. Sugar bush's leaves cup inward and look like a trough.

FLOWERS: Small, tight clusters of tiny flowers erupt from the ends of the growing branches and stems. Colors range from white and pink to burgundy. They bloom February–May.

BERRIES: Pink to rusty red, relatively flat, and about 0.25 inch in diameter, these fruits have a sticky exterior and are coated in a fine down. They form in dense clusters at the ends of branches and are easy to harvest. There is very little pulp in the fruit: it is mostly seed.

SEASON: Berries ripen mid-spring through summer.

BENEFITS: Both berries make an excellent, refreshing trail snack and a fine tea.

OTHER NAMES: Sumac

Catalina cherry   scrub oak   toyon

COMPARABLE SPECIES: While the branching structure and leaves are sometimes confused with Catalina cherry, scrub oak, and toyon, there's no comparable species with similar fruit. No other fruits are that clustered, small, and sticky.

NOTES: Berries are either eaten as a trail snack or sipped in a delightful tea. If you're eating them raw, suck the moisture from the seed, and spit out the pulp and seeds. To make tea, steep the berries in cold or warm water for up to 30 minutes and then strain it through a coffee filter or cheesecloth. Do not boil the berries, as it will make the tea sour.

MANZANITA
(Arctostaphylos spp.)

WILD

TYPE: Evergreen shrub, small tree
STATUS: Native
LEAF ARRANGEMENT: Alternate
HARVEST TIME: Spring through summer, depending on species

HABITAT: Common along the coast, throughout the coastal mountains, and as far inland as Joshua Tree National Park. They can also be found on the Channel Islands and at elevations of up to 6,500 feet in the San Bernardino Mountains. They are more abundant in areas with more than 13 inches of annual rainfall.

GROWTH: There are many types of native manzanita, and they range from a sprawling ground cover to small trees. Their most distinguishing attributes are their beautiful coral-red-to-mahogany trunks and branches, which are revealed after the bark peels and flakes off. They prefer deep, well-drained soils and struggle in urban environments, although they are commonly planted in native gardens. All produce edible fruit.

LEAVES: Thick and tough with a dusty gray-green or yellow-green color, this leaf is distinct. It is oval, elliptical, or paddle-shaped and 0.5–2 inches long. Its leaf tips are either rounded or pointed. Some leaves slightly curl or cup along the margins.

FLOWERS: Petite pink or white flowers droop from clusters at the ends of branches. Some varieties are profuse bloomers, while others are not. Flowers look like tiny vases hung upside down and are no more than 0.5 inch long. Their 5 petals are fused together. It blooms between January and June.

BERRY: About 0.5 inch in diameter, the fruit resembles a tiny apple or cherry. They dangle in clusters and start out lime green; take on red hues; turn a rich, deep red; and mature to a burnt or rust red. Some varieties are covered in a sticky goo; others aren't. Manzanita means "little apple" in Spanish.

SEASON: Early-blooming varieties produce ripe fruit in spring; the late bloomers fruit in summer.

BENEFITS: High in carbohydrates and flavor, steeped berries provide a refreshing tea.

OTHER NAMES: Kinnikinnick, bearberry

jojoba

COMPARABLE SPECIES: Jojoba can be found growing on some of the same mountains as manzanita, and the leaves look similar, but jojoba leaves are opposite, not alternate; the flowers are tiny, not showy; and the fruit looks like an acorn, not an apple.

NOTES: Ripe berries are eaten raw, brewed, cooked, or dried. Berries are steeped in boiling water for tea. Dried fruit is pounded and added to dishes, soups, and desserts. Unripe, green berries are made into teas. Seeds are dried and pounded into a meal.

Mountain grape

MOUNTAIN GRAPE AND COAST BARBERRY
(Berberis (Mahonia) aquifolium and Berberis pinnata)

WILD

TYPE: Shrub
STATUS: Native
LEAF ARRANGEMENT: Odd-pinnate
HARVEST TIME: Spring through early summer

HABITAT: Mountain grape is found in the mountains, at elevations of up to 6,500 feet. It needs moderate rainfall and acidic, deep soils. Look for it in ravines and near forest clearings. The coast barberry is found on coastal bluffs and on inner coastal mountains at elevations below 4,000 feet. There are 13 native varieties of *Berberis* and these can be found in native gardens throughout the state.

GROWTH: Both shrubs are evergreen and erect. Mountain grape is dense and grows 2–6 feet tall and almost as wide. Coast barberry can grow up to 5 feet tall, but it is generally shorter. They spread by sprouting roots.

LEAVES: The leaves of both plants are up to 1 foot long and comprised of 5–9 leaflets (odd-pinnate). Barberry is California's version of holly, and the leaflets are similar. They are distinctly toothed with tiny spines. The leaflets are oval or elliptical, shiny and stiff, and 1–3 inches long and up to 1.75 inches wide. Mountain grape's leaves are bigger; coast barberry's margins are wavier. Leaf color ranges from rich green to orange and red.

FLOWERS: Small mustard-yellow flowers cluster in dense racemes at the ends of branches. Both bloom February–May.

BERRY: Up to 0.25 inch in diameter and round or oblong, the fruit is a light purple, pale blue, or dark blue. It may be covered in a whitish film. It has a large seed.

SEASON: Spring through early summer

BENEFITS: Barberries have been used for centuries as a tonic for a variety of digestive ailments. They contain vitamin C and may have antimicrobial, antioxidant, and anti-inflammatory properties. **NOTE:** Too many berries can cause diarrhea.

OTHER NAMES: Oregon grape and shiny leaf mahonia

COMPARABLE SPECIES: None

NOTES: Fruit is eaten raw or cooked. They are sour. Flowers are edible, too, and can be eaten raw or added to teas and dishes.

NATAL PLUM
(Carissa macrocarpa)

WILD ORNAMENTAL

TYPE: Evergreen shrub
STATUS: Non-native
LEAF ARRANGEMENT: Opposite and oval
HARVEST TIME: Spring and summer

WARNING: Branches and stems have long thorns.

HABITAT: Natal plum is a staple of urban foraging. This coastal plant is native to South Africa but thrives in the city and is widely used because of its vicious thorns. You will find it on commercial and municipal properties and residential lots managed by grumpy gardeners. Stems will root when touching soil, and it has naturalized along the coast in Los Angeles, Orange, and San Diego Counties.

GROWTH: There are a number of subspecies of *C. macrocarpa*. Some are ground covers, growing to 1.5 feet tall and 6 feet wide. Others are medium-size shrubs that are 2–5 feet tall and 3–5 feet wide. The tallest natal plum can grow to nearly 10 feet tall and wide. Its primary traits are its glossy oval leaves and Y-shaped thorns that are more than 1 inch long.

LEAVES: With leaves that are shiny, forest green, and oval with smooth edges, natal plum is easy to spot. Leaves are 1–3 inches long. The leaves grow opposite of each other on strong, stout, green stems. Leaves often terminate in a tiny spine.

FLOWERS: Five pure-white elongated petals join together to create a distinct star-like flower. It has a sweet fragrance and is 0.5–1.5 inches in diameter.

BERRY: Oval, bright red to purplish red, and up to 1.5 inches long, this is a substantial fruit.

SEASON: Peak season is late spring through summer, but plants bloom intermittently throughout the year, and fruit can be found nearly all year.

BENEFITS: This fruit is abundant and rich in magnesium, phosphorus, and vitamin C.

OTHER NAMES: None

COMPARABLE SPECIES: None

NOTES: Leaves, stems, and fruit exude a milky latex sap—it is not toxic. Fruit is eaten raw or made into jelly or sauces. Make sure the fruit is soft and ripe before digging in: unripe is sour. Some people will experience an allergic reaction if they get pricked by the thorns—always wear gloves around these plants.

Douglas' Nightshade

NIGHTSHADE, WHITE
AND **DOUGLAS'**
(Solanum americanum and Solanum douglasii)

TYPE: Annual or perennial
STATUS: Native
LEAF ARRANGEMENT: Alternate, on a branch
HARVEST TIME: Summer is the peak harvest time, but they can be found almost all year

WILD

WARNING: Never, ever eat the berries if they are green—they are toxic.

HABITAT: Found widely west of the coastal ranges and sporadically in both the low and high deserts, these native species tolerate people and can be found in urban and rural canyons and clearings. While not fussy about soil pH, they need at least 10 inches of moisture per year. *S. americanum* tolerates salty soils and is found on the Channel Islands and around farms.

GROWTH: Spindly and eagerly branching, these nightshades grow between 1 and 4 feet tall and are often wider. Branches and stems are a light lime green.

LEAVES: Shaped like an arrowhead, and 1–4 inches long and up to 2.5 inches wide, leaves might have broadly toothed and/or mildly wavy margins. Leaf color ranges from forest green to pale green. Leaf stems (petioles) reach up to 1.5 inches long.

FLOWERS: Dangling in clusters of 3–6 flowers, each individual flower is less than 0.5 inch in diameter, with white to light-purple petals and bright yellow stamens. The flowers are star-like and have 5 pronounced points. Clusters (umbel) grow from along the stems. They bloom March through November.

BERRY: Round and about 0.25 inch in diameter, berries are found growing in clusters throughout a plant. Color ranges from black to dark purple and glossy to dullish.

SEASON: Berry production peaks in summer, but some plants produce intermittently throughout the year.

BENEFITS: With a taste similar to that of their relative—the tomato—these fruits have a sweet or sour taste and provide a nearly year-round snack.

OTHER NAMES: Black nightshade

COMPARABLE SPECIES: The nightshade family is huge and includes many native, invasive, and ornamental plants. It also includes many toxic members and eating them can lead to severe discomfort and even death. However, there are edible members, too, such as the tomato, potato, and eggplant. Importantly, never harvest *Solanum* unless you can positively identify the species.

NOTES: Berries are eaten raw, dried, or cooked. **SAFETY NOTE:** There are three *important* notes about these plants. First, do not eat the unripe green berries: they are toxic. Second, never assume the berries from all *Solanum* species are edible—always follow the advice of multiple experts because there are toxic species (although with much different leaves). Third, and luckily, deadly nightshade (*Atropa belladonna*) is not found in Southern California.

SERVICEBERRY
(Amelanchier spp.)

WILD

TYPE: Deciduous shrub
STATUS: Native
LEAF ARRANGEMENT: Alternate and simple
HARVEST TIME: Summer through early fall

HABITAT: Serviceberry is found in nearly all of our mountainous areas. Los Padres National Forest, San Bernardino National Forest, Cleveland National Forest, Joshua Tree National Park, Mojave National Preserve, and the Laguna Mountains all have this shrub. Typically, they need fairly deep, slightly acidic soil and are found as often in the upper scrublands as they are in the woodlands.

GROWTH: Three species of serviceberry grow here, and all lose their leaves in winter. They grow from 2.5 to 18 feet tall and often as wide. They are strong growers and create dense thickets of brittle stems. The unique leaf is serviceberry's distinguishing attribute.

LEAVES: Leaves are round, oval, or arrow-shaped, with blunt ends and 0.5–1.5 inches long and almost as wide. This leaf is unique because the upper portion has serrated margins, whereas the lower has smooth.

FLOWERS: Growing from the ends of stems on short petioles, flowers are borne in clusters of 3 to 6. Individual flowers are roughly 1 inch in diameter, have 5 widely spaced, long white petals, and the center is small and pale yellow. They bloom April through June.

BERRY: Round and ranging in size from 0.25 to 0.5 inch in diameter, serviceberries develop in small clusters. They are unripe when pale green, pink, or red; they are ripe when blue or deep purple. This summertime berry has a fringed crown at its end, making it distinct from other berries.

SEASON: Berries ripen in summer, but they still can be found dried on the shrubs early in the fall.

BENEFITS: Serviceberries have many of the same benefits as blueberries: They are an antioxidant and provide fiber, as well as minerals, sugar, and vitamins C and E.

OTHER NAMES: Western serviceberry, juneberry, Saskatoon

clematis

COMPARABLE SPECIES: Native clematis leaves and flowers somewhat resemble serviceberry, but clematis is a vine, not a shrub, and it produces no berries. Clematis flowers and leaves are slightly toxic.

NOTES: Eaten raw, dried, or cooked, serviceberry is a favorite of foragers and is relatively easy to harvest. The texture is sometimes dry and grainy, but the taste is mild, if not sweet.

STRAWBERRY, WILD
(Fragaria vesca)

WILD ORNAMENTAL

TYPE: Spreading perennial
STATUS: Native
LEAF ARRANGEMENT: Rosette
HARVEST TIME: Summer

HABITAT: Found along the coast in Santa Barbara and at elevations up to 7,500 feet in the mountains, wild strawberry prefers somewhat deep and acidic soils and moderate amounts of rainfall. It grows well in urban areas and is common in native gardens.

GROWTH: These diminutive trailing plants are a smaller version of their commercial cousins and exhibit the same leaves, berries, and trailing stems, but smaller. They grow 3–9 inches tall and 1 foot wide. The plant spreads via rooting stems (stolons), sprouting roots (rhizomes), and via seed.

LEAVES: Strawberry leaves are found at the end of 6-inch stems; they consist of 3 leaflets (trifoliate), which are thin, elliptical, or oval, 0.75–2 inches long, and have serrated edges. Leaf color ranges from rich forest green to yellow-green. The undersides of the leaves may be hairy.

FLOWERS: About 0.5 inch in diameter with 5 small white petals and a yellow center, it looks like the classic strawberry, but smaller. It blooms February–May.

BERRY: Between 0.25 and 0.5 inch in diameter, scarlet red, and dangling from the end of thin stems, these small fruits are easy to spot in summer.

SEASON: Fruit becomes ripe in summer.

BENEFITS: Berries have good amounts of iron, potassium, riboflavin, and vitamin C, as well as some sugar and vitamins A and B.

OTHER NAMES: Beach strawberry, California strawberry, wood strawberry

stinging nettle   trailing mallow

COMPARABLE SPECIES: There are two plants that resemble strawberry. Stinging nettle (*Urtica dioica*, page 90) has a similar leaf, but it only has one leaf per stem, not three leaflets. Red-flowered mallow is somewhat similar and grows along the ground, but it only has one leaf per stem, and they are positioned alternately.

NOTES: The fruit is small and tart but wonderfully satisfying. Eat it raw, dried, or cooked. Leaves, whether fresh or dried, are boiled for a tasty tea.

WATER JACKET
(Lycium andersonii)

TYPE: Shrub, drought deciduous
STATUS: Native
LEAF ARRANGEMENT: Basal on a branch, succulent leaves sprout from nodes
HARVEST TIME: Summer

WILD

WARNING: Never, ever eat the green berries—they are toxic.

HABITAT: Water jacket is not often found west of the mountains, but it is fairly common east of them. A mountainous shrub that prefers gravelly soils, it's often found in canyons, on slopes, and in desert washes. They can be found at elevations of up to 6,500 feet. Needing at least 6 inches of moisture per year, it suffers in the low desert.

GROWTH: Water jacket forms dense thickets of woody stems and sharp thorns—they can be impregnable and threatening. Such masses range from 2 to 9 feet tall and wide. Thorns are up to 0.75 inch long and grow almost perpendicularly on wildly intersecting branches. Leaves are succulent-like, clustered at the nodes, and tiny. The fruit looks like a tiny tomato.

LEAVES: Small, plump, and clustered, these leaves are unique. They look succulent and are about 0.5 inch long, thick, and oblong. Up to 5 leaves may sprout from a growing node along branches and stems. Leaf color varies between lime green, forest green, and dusty gray-green. It sheds leaves during dry spells.

FLOWERS: Water jacket's flower looks like a dainty funnel; it is almost 0.5 inch long but very narrow. Petals flair at right angles and create a star-like colorful entrance to the flower. The long throat is a light yellow-green, but the face is dusty white, lavender, or vaguely violet. Flowers form at the axis of branches and stems, and there is only one flower per node. It blooms March–May.

BERRY: The fruit looks like a tiny tomato; it is round or oval and almost 0.5 inch long. When ripe, color varies from orangish red to red. Unripe berries, which are toxic, are a pale green.

SEASON: Fruit ripens in summer.

BENEFITS: Fruit in the desert is a gift. They may be a good source of bioactive compounds and vitamins A, C, and E, as many of their cousins' berries are.

OTHER NAMES: Anderson's Wolfberry or Anderson thornbush

COMPARABLE SPECIES: The plant that most resembles water jacket is firethorn (*Pyracantha* spp.). The biggest difference is the arrangement of the berries. Pyracantha produces berries that dangle in clusters; water jacket produces berries along their stems. Firethorn berries can be eaten, but only with cooking and straining.

NOTES: Fruit is eaten raw, dried, or cooked. Flavor ranges from delicious to bitter. Never eat the unripe, pale-green berries—they are toxic.

Other Plants with Edible Berries

Saltbush, big *Atriplex lentiformis* (page 84)

MESQUITE

FRUITS

Despite their fantastic flavors, how easy they can be to find, and the thrill of eating them, wild fruit are some of the least likely species to be harvested. That's unfortunate: they are less likely to have toxins. Air and soil contaminants are often trapped or transformed as they move through a plant's vascular system, and fruits are at found at the end of the plant. Join the fun and eat up.

Using the word fruit to describe the foods below will mislead a lot of people. A fruit is the fleshy part of a plant that contains the seed. Some of the fruits below are nearly inconspicuous, others are large, but hardly edible looking. While berries are also a type of fruit, they are covered in the previous chapter (page 96).

IMPORTANT: Always rinse and clean the fruits and flowers before eating.

BLADDERPOD
(Peritoma arborea)

WILD

TYPE: Shrub

STATUS: Native

LEAF ARRANGEMENT: Alternate and trifoliate, divided into three oblong leaflets. In some cases, however, 2 or 3 leaves may sprout from one axis.

HARVEST TIME: Winter through early fall

HABITAT: Bladderpod is found throughout Southern California, except in the lowest deserts and the highest elevations. It prefers moderately deep soils and is likely to be found on bluffs, foothills, and in gravelly washes. Its tolerance of heat and salty soil helps explain bladderpod's prevalence.

GROWTH: This openly branched shrub grows 1.5–6 feet tall and almost as wide. It is twiggy, but not dense. Its most distinguishing characteristic is the smell of its crushed leaf, which some people find repulsive. You can often smell this plant before you see it.

LEAVES: Each leaf is comprised of 3 leaflets. Each leaflet is oblong, narrow, and 0.5–1.75 inches long. The leaf color is a dull to dusty green.

FLOWERS: Small flowers on tiny stems bloom en masse along a stalk (inflorescence). Stalks are 0.5–9 inches long. Flowers are tube-like when young, and then splay open with 4 petals at maturity. They are bright mustard yellow with 6 stamens erupting from the center. Bladderpod blooms November–June.

FRUIT: Translucent greenish oval sacks about 1 inch long dangle from flower stalks. They resemble an inflated bladder when young, and a paper lantern when old and dry. These pods will hang on the stems for months.

SEASON: Winter through summer

BENEFITS: The seeds contain a good amount of healthful oil and protein.

OTHER NAMES: Burrofat and California Cleome. Its botanical name was formerly *Isomeris arborea*.

COMPARABLE SPECIES: Given its unique, sulfur-like scent and translucent fruits, there are no comparable species.

NOTES: When young, the entire fruit pod can be eaten raw or cooked. As the pod matures, and the pungent flavor intensifies, the seeds are removed and eaten raw or cooked. The flavor is best described as a strong mustard-onion. The flowers are also edible, but they must be cooked to remove bitterness and toxins.

CAROB
(Ceratonia siliqua)

WILD ORNAMENTAL

TYPE: Evergreen tree
STATUS: Non-native
LEAF ARRANGEMENT: Alternate and pinnately compound; even number of leaflets, with 2 or 5 pairs
HARVEST TIME: Summer through fall

HABITAT: Carob is a widely planted ornamental tree that can be found in much of Southern California, with the exception of the high desert. It is naturalized in parts of Los Angeles and Orange Counties. It is planted for its durability, clean look, and shade, but rarely for its fruit. Carob is a commercial crop elsewhere in the world.

GROWTH: A beautiful tree that can grow to 40 feet tall and just as wide, carob's canopy is dense, making it a great shade tree and ideal for urban areas. The trunk and branches are sturdy and thick, and the bark is a flaky rich brown.

LEAVES: Long and comprised of many leaflets, carob's leaves are pinnately compound, with 2 or 5 pairs of leaflets. Total leaf length ranges from 4 to 8 inches. The oval leaflets are glossy, thick, and up to 2 inches long.

Leaflets have a pronounced midvein. Leaf color varies between lime green and a darker forest green.

FLOWERS: Almost inconspicuous masses of tiny spiraling flowers are borne on 4-inch-long clusters along branches and stems. They are red to brownish orange and stinky.

FRUIT: Female trees produce the fruit, and they are hard not to notice. The seedpods are more than 12 inches long, narrow, flat, and a dark rusty brown. The seedpods are not linear, but hook, almost like a boomerang. They dangle and litter en masse.

SEASON: Summer through fall

BENEFITS: The fruit and pulp of carob have been used for centuries to feed humans and animals. It is a common substitute for chocolate and loaded with sugar. It is delicious.

OTHER NAMES: St. John's bread

black locust

COMPARABLE SPECIES: Many trees from the pea family have similar leaf arrangements, most notably black locust (page 158). However, both the size of the fruit and delicious smell of the pulp distinguish it from all other plants.

NOTES: The pulp is sweet, refreshing, and instinctively edible. To eat it, remove the pulp from the hard shell and seeds and eat it raw. Processing the carob and creating flour or extract is common, but that is outside the scope of this book.

Catalina cherry

CHERRY, WILD
(Prunus spp.)

WILD

TYPE: Evergreen or deciduous shrubs and trees
STATUS: Native and non-native
LEAF ARRANGEMENT: Alternate and simple
HARVEST TIME: Summer and fall

HABITAT: Whether along the coast or a public park, a mountain pass or desert foothill, there is a *Prunus* species growing near you. The most commonly found and foraged species and subspecies are listed below.

Native: Desert almond (*P. fasciculate*) is found in desert washes and foothills; desert apricot (*P. fremontii*) is likely on the eastern flanks of coastal and intercoastal mountains; hollyleaf cherry (*P. ilicifolia* and *P. ilicifolia* ssp. *ilicifolia*) is very likely within 100 miles of the coast; Catalina cherry (*P. ilicifolia* ssp. *lyonii*) is somewhat likely along the coast; chokecherry (*P. virginiana* and *P.* var. *demissa*) are likely at altitude within coastal-influenced mountains

Ornamental: Carolina laurelcherry (*P. caroliniana*) is used as a hedge throughout region; English laurel (*P. laurocerasus*) is also used as a hedge, but it is not as widely planted as the former.

Invasive: Cherry plum (*P. cerasifera*) is found in urban gardens and some washes in Los Angeles, Riverside, and San Bernardino Counties.

GROWTH: While the desert varieties are low growing, most of the Prunus listed here are large shrubs or trees. The best way to identify them is to crush a leaf and smell it. If it has an almond-like scent, it is a Prunus species.

LEAVES: Large for their environment, glossy, alternate, and generally oval, oblong, or lance-like, Prunus leaves are noticeable for their rich green or lime-green color and smooth texture. There are no lobes, and leaf margins are smooth or lightly toothed.

FLOWERS: Prunus flowers are known for their 5 petals, 5 sepals, and many showy stamens. They are either tiny and cascade in tight clusters; small and bunched in groups that resemble an umbrella; or singular, large, and showy. Flower color ranges from creamy white to striking pink or pinkish red. Many flowers have a sweet almond-like fragrance. Prunus species generally bloom in spring.

FRUIT: Known as a stone fruit (drupe), the wild cherry has a large seed, just like its cousins, the almond, apricot, peach, and plum. Fruit color ranges from pink, cherry red, and maroon to blue, purple, or dusty green.

SEASON: Fruits become ripe summer through fall.

BENEFITS: Prunus fruits include riboflavin, sugars, and vitamins B6, C, and K.

OTHER NAMES: Too many to list

COMPARABLE SPECIES: There are no comparable species that are poisonous.

NOTES: Eat the fruits raw or cooked. As a rule, never eat the leaves and seeds. Both have hydrogen cyanide. In small quantities, the chemical is not toxic.

FIG, COMMON
(Ficus carica)

WILD ORNAMENTAL

TYPE: Deciduous shrub or tree
STATUS: Non-native
LEAF ARRANGEMENT: Alternate and palmate
HARVEST TIME: Late summer through fall

HABITAT: This Mediterranean invader is prevalent in and along the seeps and streams of Southern California. It can be found all along the coast, in the deserts, and at elevations of up to 5,000 feet in the mountains. The more impacted a stream is by urban influences, such as heat and pollutants, the more likely it is you'll find fig.

GROWTH: A spindly tree with lopsided growth that is between 8 and 35 feet tall and wide, the fig's trunk is either single or multi-branched. The trunk and branches are whitish, becoming gnarled with age.

LEAVES: Found on petioles (stems) that might reach 4 inches long, the leaves are large and 3–12 inches in diameter, widely oval, and either moderately or severely palmately lobed (5 lobes), although some leaves have 3 lobes or none at all. Leaf colors range from rich forest green and turf green to lime green, with a rough texture that is almost sandpaper-like.

FLOWERS: Tucked in the axis between the branches and petioles, the flowers are small, inconspicuous, and white to light green. It blooms March–April.

FRUIT: Shaped like a small avocado (obovoid), the fruit is 2–3 inches across and varies between green, yellow, red, or purple.

SEASON: Figs typically ripen summer through fall, although they will sometimes produce fruit in spring.

BENEFITS: A delicious fruit, figs are a good source of calcium, copper, iron, potassium, sugar and vitamin A.

OTHER NAMES: No other names

castor bean

COMPARABLE SPECIES: The large and lobed palmate leaves might be confused for castor bean (*Ricinus communis*, page 17). However, castor bean has toothed and pointed lobes and fig has rounded lobes. Additionally, the leaves of fig have a gritty texture; castor bean's are smooth.

NOTES: Figs are eaten raw, dried, brewed, or cooked into jams and sauces.

MALLOW
(Malva spp.)

WILD

TYPE: Annual or perennial
STATUS: Native or non-native
LEAF ARRANGEMENT: Alternate and round
HARVEST TIME: Late spring through fall

HABITAT: From the deserts and mountains to the coast and islands, *Malva* species can be found throughout Southern California. The native varieties are more likely to be found in home landscapes and botanical gardens than in the wild. The non-native varieties are found everywhere.

GROWTH: Growth varies greatly between species, ranging from 1 to 12 feet tall and 6 inches wide to 6 feet wide. While the base of the plant can get woody with age, most of the plant is fleshy and supple. Its distinguishing attributes are its ample growth and rich green, round leaves.

LEAVES: *Malva* is phototropic (its leaves turn to face the sun). The leaves are round, slightly lobed, and have serrated edges. They range from 0.5 to 4 inches wide, sit atop a long stem (petiole), and are a rich deep green or bluish gray-green.

FLOWERS: With 5 distinct petals, the flowers can be lilac, pink, white, and maybe even slightly blue. Most are streaked. They can be found at the axis between the leaf stem and the stalk. They bloom February–October.

FRUIT: Disk-like and 0.25–0.5 inch wide, the fruit resembles a tiny cheese wheel.

SEASON: Late spring through fall

BENEFITS: Fruits have protein, starch, and fiber. They provide energy and aid in digestion.

OTHER NAMES: Cheeseweed, Bull mallow, Cretan mallow, island mallow, and tree mallow

ivy

ivy geranium

COMPARABLE SPECIES: Both common and ivy geranium (*Pelargonium* spp.) might be confused with mallow when young. Both will upset your stomach if you eat them. The leaves of *Pelargonium* may have stripes or colors, and all its leaves have a distinct scent when crushed. Mallow does not have a strong smell. Ivy (*Hedera*, page 18) also has a similar-looking leaf, but its vining nature sets it apart from the mallows.

NOTES: The fruit is eaten raw or cooked. The fruit is nutty and delicious. If eating raw, remove the fibrous husk first. The fruits of all members of the genus *Malva* are edible, which includes cheeseweed (page 44) and hollyhock (page 156).

MESQUITE
(Prosopis spp.)

WILD

TYPE: Deciduous tree
STATUS: Native (with many ornamental varieties)
LEAF ARRANGEMENT: Opposite and evenly pinnate
HARVEST TIME: Summer

HABITAT: A common feature in both the Mojave and Sonoran Deserts, Mesquite has an expansive range that spans the coast of San Diego to elevations up to 4,000 feet on the eastern flanks of the mountains. Mesquite can survive in areas with very little water, growing in environments with 5 inches or less of annual rainfall.

GROWTH: From a distance mesquite looks wispy and dull, but up close it is a marvel. Its leaves look delicate; its blossoms are long, tubular, and a rich creamy yellow; and it produces an abundance of slender seedpods. Mesquite grows 10–30 feet tall and often wider. It has small sharp spines at the axis of the branches and leaf stems.

LEAVES: Mesquite leaves are long but comprised of 14–34 leaflets growing opposite of each other (evenly pinnate). The leaflets are oblong, narrow, and up to 1.5 inches long. The leaf color is a dusty grayish green to grass green.

FLOWERS: This desert tree's blossoms look like a fluffy cat's tail (raceme). They are 2–4 inches long, comprised of many minute flowers, and a creamy yellow or white. They bloom in profuse bunches. Pollinators love them. Mesquite may bloom multiple times, but it does so primarily in spring through midsummer.

FRUIT: A member of the pea family, it has distinct bean-shaped seedpods. They are 2–7 inches long, thin, and bowed or twisted. The seeds are visible as humps. Seedpods are pale green when young, and dusty yellow, tan, or reddish when brittle and mature.

SEASON: Late spring through summer

BENEFITS: Mesquite is one of the most useful trees in arid environments. Its seedpods give protein, sugars, and essential minerals; its bountiful flowers help bees produce honey; and its wood is prized for both practical and artistic endeavors.

OTHER NAMES: Honey mesquite, screw bean, Arizona mesquite

COMPARABLE SPECIES: There are no comparable species.

NOTES: The pulp inside the seedpod is eaten raw or cooked. The taste should be sweetish—discard if it's dusty or bitter. The entire pod can be dried, ground (with the fibrous material removed), and used as flour. Seeds are incredibly hard but highly nutritious.

QUICK GUIDE: It is always best to harvest pods from the tree, not the ground. Also, make sure the pod is free of injury and not discolored. Seedpods are ready to harvest when you can easily pull them off the tree—no yanking required.

ROSE, CALIFORNIA WILD
(Rosa californica)

WILD

TYPE: Deciduous (freeze and/or drought) shrub
STATUS: Native
LEAF ARRANGEMENT: Alternate and odd-pinnate
HARVEST TIME: July through January

HABITAT: This wild rose is fairly common within 80 miles of the coast. It prefers moisture and some shade and can be found in canyons and ravines, along creeks and streams, and at elevations up to 6,600 feet in the mountains, not to mention in native gardens everywhere.

GROWTH: A small sprawling shrub that reaches up to 3 feet tall in dry areas and more than 10 feet as a wildly arching plant in moist habitats, this rose spreads via seed and its rooting stems. Its long branches and stems are covered in tiny thorns. This rose may be deciduous in winter and/or summer.

LEAVES: Each leaf is comprised of 5–7 toothed leaflets. Total leaf length varies between 2 and 7 inches. Leaflets are generally oval in shape and have rounded ends. They are slightly hairy. Leaf color ranges from yellow-green to forest green.

FLOWERS: The flower is delicate to hot pink, no more than 2 inches across, and has 5 petals. These simple flowers look like butterflies sitting atop a sprawling shrub. They are slightly fragrant and bloom May–August.

FRUIT: All roses produce edible fruit, called hips. The hip of the wild rose is rarely more than 0.75 inches wide. Cherry red, but sometimes with deep orange or maroon color, a wild rose hip looks like a small, slightly oval gumball. It has an earthy fragrance. The fruit can persist on a plant for 9 months or more.

SEASON: July–January

BENEFITS: Rose hips have been used for centuries as treatments for colds, pain, and many other maladies. They are high in minerals and nutrients, including vitamins A and C, calcium, iron, and phosphorus.

OTHER NAMES: Wild rose

blackberry   raspberry   poison oak

COMPARABLE SPECIES: Other sprawling thorny plants include blackberry and raspberry, both of which have larger leaves, smaller flowers, and edible fruit. Wild roses can often be found growing alongside poison oak (page 30)—be careful.

NOTES: Rose hips are eaten raw or cooked. If eating them raw, be sure to remove the seeds and the tiny hairs that surround them—the hairs are irritants. If you boil and strain them, the seeds do not have to be removed. Like the apple seed, rose seeds have small amounts of cyanide and should be avoided. Freezing hips improves their flavor. Rose petals are also edible and have been used for centuries as a flavoring and in teas. Some people claim that rose petal tea is an analgesic. Petal flavor varies from bland to floral.

SEA FIG
(Carpobrotus chilensis, C. edulis)

WILD

TYPE: A spreading, trailing succulent
STATUS: Non-native
LEAF ARRANGEMENT: Rosette growth from trailing stems
HARVEST TIME: Late spring through early fall

HABITAT: Succulents like sea fig prefer frost-free conditions, well-drained soil, and full sun. It thrives in salty environments, which makes it easy to find anywhere along the coast, even on islands, where sea fig is highly invasive. It can also be found in the protected areas of the desert.

GROWTH: Sea fig is long-lived. It grows 4–6 inches high and many feet long. The stems take root when they touch soil. Like its fellow succulent iceplant, sea fig accumulates salt in its leaves; when the leaves die, they leave behind a saline layer that prevents most other plants from growing in that location.

LEAVES: The decisively triangular, ribbed, and plump leaves are pale green or grass green; they're reddish green when older. They are 1–3 inches long, with reddish ribs. The stems are typically a lighter green.

Leaves cluster from the stems in rosettes. The leaves of *Carpobrotus chilensis* are more reddish.

FLOWERS: Sea fig's flowers are daisy-like. They are 3–5 inches wide, with pale yellow or magenta-purple petals that are attached to a vibrant yellow center that is 1–1.5 inches wide. *Carpobrotus chilensis* has magenta petals, and *C. edulis*'s are pale yellow. Flowers originate in the axis of the leaf and stem.

FRUIT: Sitting above the foliage like a bulb, the fruit is 1–1.5 inches long and 0.5 inch wide. When immature, it is light green; when ripe and ready, it is a pale yellow. Unripe fruit is sour.

SEASON: Fruit might be found anytime between March and October. They wither in the colder months. Leaves can be harvested year-round.

BENEFITS: Sea fig might have antibacterial and anti-cancer properties, although the research is not extensive. It is best used as a thirst-quenching hiking snack.

OTHER NAMES: Hottentot fig, iceplant, cape fig, sour fig

COMPARABLE SPECIES: There are no comparable species.

NOTES: To eat this fruit, pry it open, scoop out the mucus-like pulp, and eat it, or tear off the top and squeeze the pulp out. The thick leaves are eaten in the same way, but make sure to avoid its astringent skin.

STRAWBERRY TREE
(Arbutus unedo)

ORNAMENTAL

TYPE: Evergreen tree
STATUS: Non-native
LEAF ARRANGEMENT: Alternate and simple
HARVEST TIME: Fall through winter

HABITAT: This tree is not naturalized, but it is widely planted in urbanized areas. From coastal shopping centers to desert communities, this evergreen can be found on commercial, municipal, and residential properties.

GROWTH: Strawberry tree ranges from 10 to 35 feet tall and is almost as wide. Its primary characteristics are its beautiful creamy red- to deep mahogany-colored trunk and its thin, flaking rust-brown-colored bark. This species prefers slightly acidic, well-drained soils, with only moderate moisture.

LEAVES: Oblong, oval, or elliptical in shape, the leaves are 2–3 inches long and a deep glossy green. This plant's broadleaved evergreen leaves contrast beautifully with the reddish hues of its trunk and branches. The leaves are thick, flexible, and very slightly toothed. The petioles (leaf stems) are reddish with a white midvein.

FLOWERS: Dangling in clusters from the ends of branches and stems, the flowers look like tiny vases hanging upside down. They are about 0.5 inch long and white, green, light coral, or pink. It blooms October–January.

BERRY: Shaped like small Ping-Pong balls, stop-sign red, and roughly 0.75 inch in diameter, these berries scream to be eaten. The skin is gritty, but the pulp is succulent and white to honey yellow. Unripe fruit is lime green to a light mustard yellow. It takes a year for fruit to ripen, which means that it ripens when the tree is flowering, October–January.

SEASON: Berries ripen October–January.

BENEFITS: Berries are high in sugars and vitamin C.

OTHER NAMES: None

COMPARABLE SPECIES: There are no comparable species.

NOTES: Fruit can be eaten raw or cooked into jams and sauces. Flavor ranges from bland to wonderfully sweet. Madrone (*Arbutus menziesii*) is a native cousin of the strawberry tree. It can be found growing in the wild and in urban gardens, and it also produces edible fruit, though they taste bland and earthy. Madrone's trunk and branches are similar, but it is much larger with bigger leaves.

Chaparral yucca

YUCCA
(Yucca spp. and Hesperoyucca whipplei)

WILD ORNAMENTAL

TYPE: Evergreen shrub or tree
STATUS: Native and non-native
LEAF ARRANGEMENT: Basal growth from trunks that range from short to quite tall
HARVEST TIME: Mid-spring through early summer

HABITAT: Tough and versatile, yucca can be found along the coast, in mountains at elevations up to 5,500 feet down their leeward sides, and in the most eastern parts of our region, including both the Mojave and Sonoran Deserts. Their tolerance of salty and shallow soils helps explain their wild use in urban areas.

GROWTH: All yuccas look formidable. Several varieties grow up to 30 feet tall, while others reach only 3 feet and are round and porcupine-like, with a large amount of sharp lances jutting in every direction. Yucca flower stalks, like those of agave (page 148), create perches for wildlife.

LEAVES: Yucca leaves are generally rigid, erect, and slender. Most leaves have dangerously sharp points; when punctured by the plant, some people experience an allergic reaction. Leaves range from 16 inches to over 2 feet long. They can be many shades of green: blue, dusty, or yellow.

FLOWERS: Yucca flowers are pollinated at night. Occurring in shades of white (from bright and creamy to greenish or yellowish), they are slightly fragrant, 1–2 inches across, and open widely. Bats, some birds, and moths love them. Flowers are borne on stalks that look like perches; the flowers can grow 1–14 feet tall.

FRUIT: Yucca's fruit is egg-shaped, 1–5 inches long, and 0.5–2.5 inches wide. It ranges from yellowish in color to light to dark green. Only pick the fruit that is soft, tender, and ripe; otherwise, it is unpalatable.

SEASON: Mid-spring through early summer

BENEFITS: The fruit of yucca and agave have been eaten for centuries by the indigenous peoples of Southern California. It is one of the sweetest foods found in the deserts. The banana yucca (*Y. baccata*) is the tastiest.

OTHER NAMES: Banana yucca, Chaparral yucca, Our Lord's Candle, Spanish bayonet

agave

COMPARABLE SPECIES: Agaves (page 148) are the species most often confused with yuccas. Luckily, they share some of the same edible parts: flower stalks and flowers. Agave leaves have spikes, thorns, or barbs; those of yucca only have a point at the end of the leaf.

NOTES: Yucca fruit can be eaten raw or cooked, though cooking improves the flavor. When harvesting yucca, timing is critical: if the fruit is too young or too old, the fleshy parts are unpalatable. Yucca fruit has a lot of seeds, and they should be removed. Typically, fruits are roasted for 20 minutes, broken open, the seeds are scooped out, and the remaining fruit is either eaten as is or added to another dish. Yucca's flower stalk, flower petals, and dried/roasted seeds are also edible.

Other Plants with Edible Fruits

Agave *Agave* spp. (page 148)

Cattail *Typha* spp. (page 42)

Chickweed *Stellaria media* (page 66)

Dandelion *Taraxacum* spp. (page 46)

Locust, honey *Gleditsia triacanthos* (page 184)

Mustard *Brassica* spp. (page 54)

Nasturtium *Tropaeolum majus* (page 56)

Pineapple guava *Feijoa sellowiana* (page 160)

Prickly pear *Opuntia* spp. (page 58)

Radish, wild *Raphanus sativus* (page 60)

Sea rocket *Cakile* spp. (page 228)

Shepherd's purse *Capsella bursa-pastoris* (page 200)

CAROB TREE WITH CAROBS

WESTERN REDBUD

FLOWERS

Foraging flowers is a fantastic delight. Always engaging and fun to see up close, flowers are generally found near the end of a stem, which means they are farther away from the soil and may have fewer toxins than greens. When it comes to flowers, the only real disadvantage is the presence of insects.

IMPORTANT: Let your harvested flowers sit 20 minutes before you wash them; this allows the insects to flee.

AGAVE
(Agave spp.)

ORNAMENTAL

TYPE: Succulent perennial shrub; evergreen
STATUS: Native and non-native
LEAF ARRANGEMENT: Basal leaves and a central flower stalk
HARVEST TIME: Mostly late spring and summer, but some bloom any time of year

WARNING: Sap from the leaves can cause skin rashes and discomfort—wear gloves and long sleeves when working with these plants.

HABITAT: Agave is not widespread in wild areas, but it is very common in urbanized areas. Whether growing naturally or planted, this distinct cactus-like plant can be found all along the coast, at elevations up to 4,000 feet in the mountains, and throughout the deserts. It does best in coarse soils.

GROWTH: Agave's succulent tough leaves sprout from a central clump and radiate in every direction, creating a dangerous plant that resembles a giant pincushion. A few species, such as *A. americana* and *A. vilmoriniana*, have leaves that twist and turn and grow erratically.

LEAVES: Agave leaves are lethal. Many have thorns or barbs along their edges and all have a pronounced point that is as sharp as a needle. Leaves can puncture skin and, in extreme cases, sometimes break off, staying in the body. Leaves are typically thick, bulbous at the base, and long. Leaf color ranges from dusty green or gray-green to bluish and pale green with yellow streaks. Leaf length varies between 6 inches and 6 feet.

FLOWERS: Erupting from clusters on tall flower stalks that act as perches for wildlife, agave blooms look much like those of Yucca. The flower spikes grow between 6 and 40 feet tall. Agaves are monocarpic, which means they bloom once during their life and die after doing so, although it may take decades before a plant blooms. Each plant can produce many pounds of flowers.

SEASON: Agaves mostly bloom in late spring and summer, but some bloom any time of year.

BENEFITS: Agave flowers have been eaten for centuries.

OTHER NAMES: Blue agave, century plant, desert agave, Nevada agave, octopus agave, Parry's agave, and Utah agave

yucca

COMPARABLE SPECIES: Yucca is the plant most often mistaken for agave. Yucca leaves are long and narrow, not thick and wide. Most agave leaves have thorns or barbs, while yucca leaves do not.

NOTES: The petals of the flowers are removed and boiled, dried, roasted, or steamed and then added to a variety of dishes. The flavor is musty, tangy, or bland. The young flower stalks (rich in sugar) are also edible, as are flower buds and seeds, which are dried and crushed to make flour. The flower spikes are roasted or baked.

CITRUS
(Citrus spp.)

ORNAMENTAL

TYPE: Evergreen small tree
STATUS: Non-native
LEAF ARRANGEMENT: Alternate and simple
HARVEST TIME: Late winter through spring

HABITAT: *Citrus* is a genus that includes trees that produce a variety of familiar fruit, including orange, lemon, lime, grapefruit, and kumquat. Citrus trees are iconic in Southern California and can be found planted throughout the region. Citrus trees don't endure prolonged freezes, and they are rare at elevations above 2,000 feet and in unprotected areas of the desert.

GROWTH: Generally, citrus trees are small and between 8 and 30 feet tall and wide. A single trunk bears many stout branches. Some species, like lemons, have nasty thorns on their branches and stems. To identify a citrus tree, look for creamy white fragrant flowers, scented leaves, and rich green leaves.

LEAVES: Citrus leaves vary greatly in size. The kumquat's leaves are 2 inches long, narrow, and oblong, whereas Eureka lemon leaves can grow to 5 inches long and 3 inches wide. Most citrus leaves have a sweet citrusy fragrance when crushed, and all are a glossy grass green to deep green.

FLOWERS: Citrus flowers are creamy white and star-shaped with 5 petals that curl away from the center; they have tiny yellow stamens at their centers. The flowers are wonderfully fragrant.

SEASON: Late winter through spring

BENEFITS: Citrus flowers have been eaten for centuries. They are said to have a calming effect. Their essential oils are also known to be commercially extracted.

OTHER NAMES: There are many names for the various types of citrus.

COMPARABLE SPECIES: With its fragrant leaves and flowers, there are no comparable species.

NOTES: Typically, citrus trees produce a mass of flowers, many of which fall to the ground. Flowers are eaten raw, slightly cooked, or brewed into teas and extracts. The flowers are semi-sweet with a rich floral, citrusy flavor. The flowers most commonly eaten are those of orange, lemon, lime, grapefruit, and kumquat.

CLOVER
(Trifolium spp.*)*

TYPE: Annual and perennial herb
STATUS: Native and non-native
LEAF ARRANGEMENT: Trifoliate
HARVEST TIME: May through August

WILD ORNAMENTAL

HABITAT: Whether intentionally used as a ground cover or naturally growing in the wild, clover can be found throughout California—there are more than 80 different species found in the state. Although clovers prefer moderate rainfall, some humidity, and slightly acidic soils, they can be found in the deserts too.

GROWTH: Whenever possible, harvest non-native clovers; the 4 most prevalent non-native species are: red clover, rose clover, strawberry clover, and white clover (*T. pratense, T. hirtum, T. fragiferum,* and *T. repens,* respectively). These clovers are generally low-growing, spread via fleshy rooting stems, and form mats. Their distinguishing attributes are their classic trefoil leaflets and burr-like blossoms.

LEAVES: Clover leaves are comprised of 3 leaflets (occasionally 4) and sit at the end of a long and lazy-looking stem. Leaflets are generally oval and have a point. The leaf color ranges from lime green to rich deep green and many leaves may be discolored.

FLOWERS: Burr-like and bursting with tiny tubular flowers, clover flower heads are generally elongated and up to 1 inch wide. Flower heads are comprised of a mass of long-throated flowers that resemble petite pea flowers. Some flower heads are ball-shaped. Color varies between pink, red, light violet, pinkish white, and yellow.

SEASON: Blooming season varies by species. Of the non-native species, rose clover blooms February–March, strawberry in May–June, and the red and white varieties bloom between May and August.

BENEFITS: Clover has been eaten and used for centuries around the world.

OTHER NAMES: There are a wide variety of common names for the various species.

sourgrass   black medick

COMPARABLE SPECIES: Two plants resemble clover: Sourgrass (*Oxalis* spp., page 202) and black medick (*Medicago lupulina*, page 176). Luckily, all parts of sourgrass are edible. The leaves and seeds of black medick are edible, but they should be cooked first. Although black medick has the familiar trefoil and oval leaflets, it grows to 20 inches high, has stouter stems, and the flower is mustard yellow, not pastel as in the four non-native clover species.

NOTES: Pull the petals from the flower head and eat them raw, lightly cooked, or brewed into teas. Flavor ranges from grass-like and tart to semi-sweet.

HENBIT
(Lamium amplexicaule)

WILD

TYPE: Annual herb
STATUS: Non-native
LEAF ARRANGEMENT: Basal in youth, opposite and sheathed on older stems
HARVEST TIME: Midwinter through early summer

HABITAT: Henbit is easy to find in the foothills of the mountains within 80 miles of the coast. It is common around farms, roadways, and urban landscapes, but it is uncommon right along the coast and rare at elevations above 5,000 feet and farther east than Palm Springs and Anza-Borrego Desert State Park.

GROWTH: A member of the mint family, henbit has many of its familiar characteristics: square stems, sprawling growth, and colorful blooms. It is 4–16 inches tall and often much wider. Stems are slightly hairy, turn purple with age, and root when they touch the ground. Its most distinct features are its two upper leaves, which clasp the stem and create a cup-like shape; blossoms develop from this cup.

LEAVES: Henbit leaves are handsome. They are forest green and round to heart-shaped, with lobed, scalloped edges. They grow oppositely, are slightly wrinkled, and 0.3–1 inch wide.

FLOWERS: Small and tubular, henbit flowers bloom in rings above cup-shaped leaves. They are about 0.5 inch long and pink, purple, and/or violet. The lower lip of the flower is wide, lobed, and spotted. It blooms February–September.

SEASON: The greens are best when young, from midwinter through mid-spring. The flowers are eaten midwinter through late summer.

BENEFITS: Boasting chlorophyll, fiber, and many vitamins, henbit is a healthy green to eat.

OTHER NAMES: Giraffe head, henbit deadnettle

COMPARABLE SPECIES: The plant that most resembles henbit is ground ivy (*Glechoma hederacea*). Although ground ivy is uncommon and produces a sky-blue flower, it is also edible.

ground ivy

NOTES: Flowers can be eaten raw. Young leaves and stems are eaten raw or cooked and are mostly used in salads and soups. Unlike other members of the mint family, henbit's leaves aren't spicy, tasting instead a bit like earth or soil.

HOLLYHOCK
(Alcea rosea)

WILD ORNAMENTAL

TYPE: Biennial/perennial
STATUS: Non-native
LEAF ARRANGEMENT: Alternate
HARVEST TIME: May–August

HABITAT: Hollyhock is found in residential landscapes throughout Southern California, including in Big Bear, on Catalina Island, and in Palm Desert. A reliable self-seeder, the plant has naturalized and small colonies can be found in every county.

GROWTH: A profusion of brilliant flowers grows from stalks that can reach 9 feet tall; the flowers can reach 6 inches wide and sway proudly. Despite its height, the plant rarely grows wider than 2 feet. The stalks and stems are slightly hairy. Hollyhock's most distinguishing attributes are its tall flower stalks and its many large, colorful, roundish flowers.

LEAVES: Hollyhock's leaves are large, round to heart-shaped, and have a coarse texture. A rich, dark green, the leaves are 2–6 inches in diameter and may have 5–7 slightly pointed lobes (weakly palmate).

FLOWERS: A member of the mallow family, hollyhock's flowers have 5 distinct petals. Most petals are a dark red, but they may also be apricot, pink, dark purple, off white, or dull yellow. Most flowers are 3–5 inches in diameter, but they can get as wide as 6 inches; flowers grow on stems that emerge from the axis between the stalk and the leaf stem. They bloom from May through August.

SEASON: May through August

BENEFITS: These flowers have been eaten for centuries.

OTHER NAMES: No other names

ivy   ivy geranium   mallow

COMPARABLE SPECIES: Both common and ivy geranium (*Pelargonium* spp.) might be confused with hollyhock—both will upset your stomach if eaten. The leaves of *Pelargonium* may have stripes or colors, and all leaves have a distinct scent when crushed. Hollyhock does not have a strong smell. Other mallows (*Malva* spp.) are often confused with hollyhock. If you make that mistake, don't worry—all mallows are edible. Ivy (*Hedera*, page 18) also has a similar-looking leaf, but its vining nature sets it apart from hollyhock.

NOTES: Petals can be eaten raw or lightly cooked. Leaves are eaten raw or cooked; the texture is coarse.

LOCUST, BLACK
(*Robinia pseudoacacia*)

WILD ORNAMENTAL

TYPE: Deciduous tree
STATUS: Non-native
LEAF ARRANGEMENT: Pinnately compound (odd), with up to 9 pairs of leaflets
HARVEST TIME: March–June

HABITAT: Whether intentionally planted or found naturally growing in human-impacted wildlands, black locust is found throughout California. It tolerates compacted and acidic soils and drought. It grows well alongside human development.

GROWTH: Generally, this deciduous tree is twice as tall as it is wide, but at maturity it can be 75 feet tall and 60 feet wide. Its defining characteristics are its thorny branches and its long leaf, which can be comprised of up to 19 small leaflets. Its bark is a dark muddy gray, twisted, and deeply grooved.

LEAVES: Masses of long dangling leaves erupt from trunks, branches, and stems. The leaf is comprised of up to 9 pairs of leaflets and a terminating leaflet (pinnately compound, odd). Leaflets are 1–2 inches long and mostly oblong. Leaflet color changes with the season: In early spring, they are a light green, turning to a rich green in early summer and a dull mustard yellow in fall.

FLOWERS: Locust flowers are beautiful. A member of the pea family, locust trees produce a mass of showy flowers that resemble those of beans and peas. The black locust produces masses of dense flower clusters 4–8 inches long. Each flower is no more than 0.75 inch wide, rich creamy white, and has the classic lips of the pea flower: the lower and upper lips split apart widely, providing both a landing pad and a backboard for pollinators.

FRUIT: The fruit is 4 inches long, narrow, thin, and oblong if not slightly curved; it is reddish brown to dark dirty brown. They dangle en masse.

SEASON: March through June

BENEFITS: Locust flowers have been eaten for centuries. They are reputed to have calming and laxative effects.

OTHER NAMES: False Acacia

carob   mesquite

COMPARABLE SPECIES: The leaf and fruit of other pea family trees, including carob (page 126) and mesquite (page 134), are somewhat similar. The carob's flowers are almost inconspicuous and inedible. The mesquite's flowers are edible.

NOTES: Do not eat the black locust's bark, leaves, or seedpods, as all are toxic. Flowers are eaten raw, or cooked or added to dishes. They taste sweet, floral, and honey-like. Make sure there are no insects in the flowers before eating.

PINEAPPLE GUAVA
(*Feijoa sellowiana*)

ORNAMENTAL

TYPE: Evergreen shrub or tree
STATUS: Non-native
LEAF ARRANGEMENT: Opposite
HARVEST TIME: Spring

HABITAT: This ornamental tree is grown throughout Southern California. It is the hardiest of the subtropical guavas. Found in areas of the desert without a persistent freeze, the lower foothills, and in coastal communities, it is common on residential properties, around shopping centers, and in public areas.

GROWTH: Generally a small multi-branched tree, it is sometimes trained to form a single trunk. This evergreen grows 15–25 feet tall and often as wide. Without maintenance, its interior gets dense and twiggy. The tree grows gnarled with age.

LEAVES: The underside of this tree's leaves makes it distinct: they are silver-gray and shimmer in rising or fading light. Leaves are oval, 2–3 inches long, and leathery. Their top sides are dull green to glossy green.

FLOWERS: Showy, colorful, and profuse, the flowers are as delicious as they are beautiful. A mass of scarlet stamens topped with yellow pollen erupts from bright white petals that are highlighted with lilac. They are about 1 inch across.

FRUIT: Shaped like a tiny pear, the fruit is 1–3 inches long and bluish green. It matures in fall and is sweetish, gooey, and pineapple-tart.

SEASON: Spring

BENEFITS: Although these flowers have been eaten for centuries, there is little data on the amounts of vitamins and minerals.

OTHER NAMES: Feijoa

COMPARABLE SPECIES: There are no comparable species.

NOTES: The flower is eaten raw, whether by itself or added to dishes, such as salads. Cooking greatly reduces its aesthetic appeal and flavor. It is sweet with hints of pineapple and sage. Eat the stamens, petals, and ovary, but not its fibrous base and stem. Many people swear the flowers taste better than the fruit.

Yellow Evening Primrose

PRIMROSE, EVENING
(Oenothera elata ssp. and *O. speciosa)*

WILD

TYPE: Biennial or perennial
STATUS: Native and non-native
LEAF ARRANGEMENT: Rosette
HARVEST TIME: June–September

HABITAT: While there are many evening primroses in California, two are dominant: the non-native perennial Mexican evening primrose (*O. speciosa*) and the native biennial yellow evening primrose (*O. elata* ssp.). The non-native species is easy to find along the coast, up to 2,000 feet in the mountains and as far east as the Mojave Desert and Joshua Tree National Park. It is also well adapted to urban conditions. The native species is found along the coast and at elevations of up to 8,000 feet in the mountains; although rare in dry areas, it can be found in the moist areas of the Mojave and Sonoran Deserts.

GROWTH: The non-native variety grows 1 foot tall and colonizes an area via its spreading roots (rhizomes) that sprout new plants. Once rooted, it sends out many fleshy stems (rosette) that can trail up to 3 feet. The native species is biennial, with the first year spent in rosette form about

1 foot across and the second year sending up a beautiful flower stalk that can reach 4 feet tall.

LEAVES: The non-native species has leaves that are 1–3 inches long, oblong or elliptical in shape, and slightly toothed along the margins. The native species has leaves that are lance-like or oblong and 2–4 inches long, with mostly smooth margins.

FLOWERS: This plant earns its name by blooming mainly at night, attracting bats, birds, and moths. Both flowers have 4 large, heart-shaped petals, which are fragrant. The non-native species has pastel pink to light rose-colored flowers. The native species' flower is a lackluster yellow, is up to 2 inches across, and blooms along stalks that grow to 5 feet tall. The non-native variety flowers May–September; the native blooms June–September.

SEASON: June–September

BENEFITS: Primrose is reported to have healthy amounts of beta-carotene, calcium, potassium, and sugars.

chicory   dandelion   hedge mustard   sheep sorrel   shepherd's purse

OTHER NAMES: Mexican evening primrose and Hooker's evening primrose

COMPARABLE SPECIES: The plants that most resemble evening primrose are edible. These include young chicory (page 196), dandelion (page 46), hedge mustard, sheep sorrel (page 86), and shepherd's purse (page 200).

NOTES: Petals are eaten raw or lightly cooked and are sweet and delicious. Young leaves, shoots, and seeds are also edible.

REDBUD, WESTERN
(Cercis occidentalis)

WILD

TYPE: Small, multi-branched, deciduous tree
STATUS: Native
LEAF ARRANGEMENT: Alternate and simple
HARVEST TIME: February–April

HABITAT: Western redbud is a native species that's found in the wild, but it's also commonly planted in urban areas. You can find it from Santa Barbara and Lancaster to Palm Springs and Chula Vista. This foothill tree survives, if not thrives, in urban conditions.

GROWTH: Considered a large shrub or a small tree, it ranges in size from 10 to 18 feet tall and wide. Specimens with multiple trunks growing from the base are more common than those with a single trunk. A cool-season grower, redbud is one of the first native trees to bloom. It tolerates shallow soils, acidic conditions, and temperatures that dip below freezing but rarely stay there.

LEAVES: Almost fragile-looking, redbud leaves are round and 2–4 inches wide. Some leaves have a point, while others don't. Leaf color changes with the season: they are light green in spring, bluish green in summer, and a dirty yellow to red in fall.

FLOWERS: Redbud's flower is beautiful, colorful, and looks like that of a pea blossom. It is magenta to pink, has the classic pea-like wings and keel, and is about 0.5 inch wide. They bloom in profusion along stems before the tree has fully leafed out. Redbud blooms February–April.

FRUIT: Seedpods develop in summer and look like those of members of the pea family: long, narrow, thin, and reddish brown. Seedpods are 2–3 inches long. They dangle and clatter on the tree long after the tree has lost its leaves in fall—it is very distinct.

SEASON: February–April

BENEFITS: Flowers have been eaten for centuries by Native Americans and are high in vitamin C.

OTHER NAMES: Redbud

COMPARABLE SPECIES: Redbud is a small tree, blooms early, and has delicate-looking leaves, so nothing else resembles it except for the related eastern redbud, which is just as edible.

NOTES: Petals are eaten raw or lightly cooked or added to dishes. They are tart but taste good. Immature seedpods and seeds are cooked and eaten. Young leaves are edible and eaten raw or cooked. The eastern redbud (*C. canadensis*) also has edible petals and leaves. When its bark is brewed, it produces a coral-colored dye.

SAGE
(Salvia spp.)

WILD

TYPE: Annual, biennial, or perennial shrub; some are summer deciduous

STATUS: Native and non-native

LEAF ARRANGEMENT: Opposite

HARVEST TIME: March–July

HABITAT: There are around 23 wild *Salvia* species growing in Southern California. And there are more than triple that when you factor in all of the ornamental varieties. There is no shortage of *Salvia* flowers in the state. By far the sweetest is the hummingbird sage (*S. spathacea*), and it can be found in native gardens within 100 miles of the coast.

GROWTH: From varieties that form as a low-growing ground cover to shrubs that reach 10 feet high, there is an enormous variation between sages. They all share some general characteristics: square stems, narrow, paddle-like leaves, and small, colorful, long-throated flowers.

LEAVES: The leaves are commonly fragrant and generally oblong or oval. They are mostly long and narrow, but a few are big and broad. Leaves are 1–6 inches long. Most are thick, slightly hairy or fuzzy, and textured.

Sages that are well-adapted to habitats with higher moisture levels are a rich green; those adapted to sun and drought are a dusty gray-green, silver green, or nearly white.

FLOWERS: Sage flowers are generally throated, much longer than they are wide, and have a protruding lower lip that curls away from the flower. Stamens jutting from the interior reach above the flower. Some sages bloom in dense clusters (inflorescence) while others produce a few flowers in a whorl along their stems. Color varies greatly among sage species: blue, orange, pink, purple, red, salmon, scarlet, white, and yellow.

SEASON: You have a good chance of finding *Salvia* flowers between February and August; you have a great chance between March and July.

BENEFITS: *Salvia* flowers are abundant, plentiful, and interesting. Whether sweet or musty, floral or pungent, every flower is a treat.

OTHER NAMES: There are many names for sages, and the ones with the tastiest flowers are black, Cleveland, garden, hummingbird, pineapple, purple, and Sonoma.

COMPARABLE SPECIES: With incredible variation between species, positive identification is essential when eating *Salvia* flowers. Luckily, some of the plants confused with the *Salvia* produce edible flowers as well. These plants include basil, horehound, lavender, mint, rosemary, and thyme.

NOTES: Sage flowers are mostly eaten fresh, although they can be dried and used in teas and dishes as seasoning.

THISTLE, MILK
(Silybum marianum)

WILD

TYPE: Annual or perennial herb
STATUS: Non-native
LEAF ARRANGEMENT: Basal, with a central flower stalk
HARVEST TIME: April–July

HABITAT: Requiring at least 12 inches of rainfall per year, this short-lived plant is common along the parts of our region influenced by the coasts, and that includes the western flanks of the mountains and elevations up to 6,000 feet. The presence of milk thistle is typically a sign that an area has been heavily grazed; it grows well in shallow, salty soils.

GROWTH: Fleshy, reaching, and lethal, thanks to its prickles, milk thistle is distinctive for its spiny and white-splotched leaves. It grows from 6 inches to 2 feet wide and its flower stalk can reach 9 feet tall. Every part of the plant is prickly.

LEAVES: Clasping onto a stem, the leaves are oblong or paddle-shaped and 3–12 inches long. Leaf edges (margins) can be lobed, wavy, or lined, and they have many sharp spines. The wild white splotches on the upper side of the leaves make them completely unique—it looks like someone spilled milk or paint on them.

FLOWERS: Swaying from the ends of tall stalks, this flower resembles a small version of the artichoke flower (artichokes are a domesticated thistle species). Roughly 2 inches wide and with spines all around its base, the bloom is lilac purple to bluish purple and erupts from the top. It blooms April–July.

SEASON: Harvest blooms at the peak of flowering, sometime between April and July.

BENEFITS: Thistles have kept desperate pioneers alive for hundreds of years. Whether the leaves or roots, fleshy stalks or flower heads, the milk thistle has something to provide.

OTHER NAMES: Blessed milkthistle

COMPARABLE SPECIES: With its spiny leaves, splotched discoloration, and distinct flower head, milk thistle only resembles other thistles (but none have the white markings).

NOTES: Pick flower heads when flowering peaks, then boil them, scoop the heart out, and eat it like an artichoke, with butter, salt, and anything else. Young greens are also eaten raw or lightly cooked. The young stalks are treated like asparagus, and the roots can be boiled and eaten as a starch.

FLOWERS

VIOLET
(Viola spp.)

ORNAMENTAL

TYPE: Perennial herb
STATUS: Native and non-native
LEAF ARRANGEMENT: Basal growth with simple leaves
HARVEST TIME: January–May

HABITAT: Even though there are 17 native *Viola* species in Southern California, you are more likely to encounter a pair of non-native species: English violet (*V. odorata*) and pansy (*V. tricolor*). Most violets inhabit mixed evergreen or deciduous forests. They are more likely to be found in partial shade and areas with light moisture levels and plenty of nutrients. They grow well in urban landscapes and can be found all along the coast, at elevations of up to 5,000 feet in the mountains, and even in the protected pockets of the desert.

GROWTH: Low-growing, fleshy, and attractive, most *Violas* are identified by their tiny colorful flowers and heart-shaped leaves. Some violets spread by stolons (aboveground stems) and most are good at self-seeding. You will not find them in dry gardens.

LEAVES: Ranging from small and bluish green to large and rich green, leaf shape and color among violets varies greatly. The common English violet has leaves shaped like a perfect heart, which are deeply veined and a rich, enticing green. They sprout from a fleshy base, are between 0.75 and 2 inches wide, and sit atop thin stems that can reach 5 inches long.

FLOWERS: *Viola* flowers are beautiful, engaging, and delicious. They have 5 tepals (petals and sepals) that splay outward, creating both a landing pad and a backboard for small pollinators. Flower size ranges from just under 0.5 inch to 2 inches wide. The common English violet is a royal purple, but other flowers are lavender, yellow, creamy white, or violet.

SEASON: The English violet blooms January–May. Pansy blooms both early spring and late fall.

BENEFITS: *Viola* flowers have been eaten for centuries. The leaves have anti-inflammatory and laxative effects. With their beautiful, delicate flowers and heart-shaped leaves, violet has long been associated with love and romance.

OTHER NAMES: Sweet violet, common violet

creeping wild ginger

COMPARABLE SPECIES: Creeping wild ginger (*Asarum caudatum*) is native to Northern California and has been used as an ornamental species in Southern California. Like the common violet, it's found in the shade, is low-growing, and has heart-shaped leaves. However, wild ginger's flowers are vastly different: they look like a three-pronged star and are a blood red or brownish red. The leaves of wild ginger should be considered inedible.

NOTES: *Viola* flowers are eaten raw, added to dishes, or cooked. They can also be made into candy. They have a sweet floral taste that's almost honey-like. The leaf and flower bud are also edible.

Other Plants with Edible Flowers

Alfalfa, black medick, and bur clover *Medicago sativa, M. lupulina,* and *M. polymorpha* (page 176)

Bladderpod *Peritoma arborea* (page 124)

Bulrush *Bolboschoenus* spp. and *Schoenoplectus* spp. (page 212)

Cattail *Typha* spp. (page 42)

Dandelion *Taraxacum* spp. (page 46)

Dayflower and small leaf spiderwort *Commelina benghalensis* and *Tradescantia fluminensis* (page 68)

Elderberry, black and blue *Sambucus nigra* and *S. nigra* ssp. *caerulea* (page 102)

Fennel, sweet *Foeniculum vulgare* (page 48)

Filaree, red-stemmed *Erodium cicutarium* (page 50)

Mustard *Brassica* spp. (page 54)

Nasturtium *Tropaeolum majus* (page 56)

Radish, wild *Raphanus sativus* (page 60)

Rose, California wild *Rosa californica* (page 136)

Sea fig *Carpobrotus chilensis, C. edulis* (page 138)

Sourgrass *Oxalis pes-caprae* (page 202)

Sow thistle *Sonchus* spp. (page 88)

Thistle, bull *Cirsium vulgare* (page 206)

Yucca *Yucca* spp. (page 142)

CITRUS

BLACK WALNUT

SEEDS

Seeds are Southern California's summer-through-fall crop. They are generally tasty and high in carbohydrates, protein, and many essential minerals and nutrients. Our urban and wild landscapes offer a buffet of health and fun.

IMPORTANT: Always wash your seeds before consuming.

Alfalfa

Bur clover

ALFALFA, BLACK MEDICK, AND **BUR CLOVER**
(Medicago sativa, Medicago lupulina, and *Medicago polymorpha)*

WILD

TYPE: Annual, perennial herb
STATUS: Non-native
LEAF ARRANGEMENT: Alternate and trifoliate
HARVEST TIME: Late summer and early fall

HABITAT: The three most common *Medicago* species are weeds: Alfalfa, black medick, and bur clover. Alfalfa is the least common species in our area, but it is more tolerant of salts and found more often near grazing animals. Black medick and bur clover prefer slightly acidic soils and are common in and around urban areas. All three tolerate poor soils and are far more common within 100 miles of the coast. They require at least 9 inches of rainfall per year, making them uncommon in the deserts.

GROWTH: Rambling and scrambling on straight-jointed stems, these three species are either low-growing or spindly and erect. They can grow up to 3 feet tall and wide. Related to clover, their leaves have 3 leaflets. The stems are slightly hairy. To differentiate it from other 3-leaved plants, look for its spindly stems that are joined at odd angles.

LEAVES: Clover-like, these plants have leaves comprised of 3 oval leaflets (trifoliate). Unlike clover, the middle leaflet extends outward on a stem, making it look unusual. Leaf edges may be slightly toothed, if not bristly. The leaf may be creased down the middle and is a rich, deep green.

FLOWERS: Alfalfa blossoms are cone-shaped, elongated, and comprised of many small rich lavender-to-purple-colored flowers. Resembling small orbs, black medick and bur clover blossoms are comprised of many small bright-yellow flowers. Both flowers have the classic pea flower shape with an extended landing pad and a big backboard for small pollinators. Alfalfa and black medick bloom June–August; bur clover blooms February–June.

SEED: Seeds look like tiny coiled bundles and are less than 0.25 inch in length. Bur clover's seedpods are ball-like and have tiny hooked barbs. The seeds are light tan to dark brown.

SEASON: Summer and early fall

BENEFITS: Seeds are high in carbohydrates, protein, and many vitamins. The young leaves and stalks of alfalfa are a superfood, and the others are healthy as well. These plants have been eaten for centuries.

OTHER NAMES: Bur medick

clover

COMPARABLE SPECIES: The plants that resemble Medicago most have trifoliate leaves: Clover (*Trifolium* spp. page 152) and sourgrass (*Oxalis pes-caprae*, page 200). Both are lower-growing and just as edible.

NOTES: Seeds are dried or roasted and ground to make meal or mush. Very young leaves and shoots can be eaten raw. Older leaves and stems should be cooked first via boiling, sautéing, or steaming. The flowers are also edible and eaten raw or cooked.

AMARANTH
(Amaranthus spp.)

WILD

TYPE: Annual herb
STATUS: Native and non-native
LEAF ARRANGEMENT: Alternate and simple
HARVEST TIME: Late summer through fall

HABITAT: Amaranth is found throughout Southern California. The non-native species are more likely found in or near agricultural areas, near waterways, and in urban landscapes. The native species are tougher, lower growing, and can be found at elevations up to 5,500 feet and into the desert. Amaranths are scarce in the low desert.

GROWTH: Scrambling across the ground or taking the form of erect, slightly branching plants that can reach 3 feet tall, this group of species is diverse. Ornamental varieties can grow up to 6 feet tall. Stems are fleshy and mostly green, but a few are purplish or yellowish. Leaves are generally small and thick. Their most distinguishing characteristic is their flower/ seed spikes. They produce spears of nondescript flowers that turn to seeds that are golden, orange, or rusty red when mature.

LEAVES: Leaves are generally oval-shaped. The more durable and lower-growing amaranths have smaller and more linear leaves. Leaf size ranges 0.33–5 inches long and 0.12–2.5 inches wide. Veins are usually indented and noticeable.

FLOWERS: Most species bloom at the end of a stalk in a spiked cluster. Flowering spikes range from 1 to 6 inches long. A couple of species bloom along the stalk. Flowers are tiny, lack petals, and are generally yellow or dull green. Several varieties have light pink flowers.

SEED: The seeds are a dark, rich brownish black and smooth and shiny when mature and ready to harvest. They are rarely longer than 0.33 inch and are elliptical or ovate.

SEASON: Most *Amaranth* species produce seeds in late summer through fall.

BENEFITS: Amaranth has been a staple all over the world for millennia. Highly nutritious, it boasts potassium, protein, and vitamins B and E.

OTHER NAMES: Rough pigweed, redroot

stinging nettle   brittlebush   nightshade   lambsquarters   goosefoot

COMPARABLE SPECIES: The leaf can be mistaken for those of stinging nettle, but the difference is in the leaves' edges: stinging nettle has distinctly serrated leaves. Brittlebush (*Encelia* spp.) looks similar when young, but brittlebush is full of resins and smells awful. Nightshade (Douglas', white, see page 114) also has a similar leaf, and its leaf is poisonous if uncooked. Nightshade's leaves have a smooth edge, and it has pretty, nearly ever-blooming flowers. And lastly, it resembles lambsquarters and goosefoot (*Chenopodium* spp., page 52), which are closely related and highly nutritious.

NOTES: Seeds are separated from dry stalks by thrashing. They are generally hard and need to be pounded into flour before use. The flour is used in breads and soups. The young leaves are eaten raw; old leaves are cooked like spinach.

BUCKWHEAT
(Eriogonum fasciculatum and *Eriogonum fasciculatum* vars.)*

WILD

TYPE: Shrub; summer deciduous
STATUS: Native
LEAF ARRANGEMENT: Basal leaves at nodes
HARVEST TIME: Late summer through fall

HABITAT: California buckwheat (*E. fasciculatum*) and its four other varieties are wildly abundant within 110 miles of the coast and common in areas farther east that get more than 7 inches of rain per year. Buckwheat is fairly common in urban communities along the coast.

GROWTH: Generally, this species of buckwheat grows 2–5 feet tall and 2–6 feet wide. They can be compact and dense or sprawling and open. Their most distinguishing attributes are their small blade-like leaves, which grow in bunches, and their beautiful and abundant blooms.

LEAVES: Shaped like a tiny blade, the leaves are narrow, elliptical, and flat. They burst forth in clusters from nodes along extended stems. They are about 0.5 inch long and 0.12 inch wide. Leaves are grass green to deep green, leathery, and woolly. The plant is drought deciduous (it loses leaves during periods of drought).

FLOWERS: Buckwheat flowers look like drops of ice cream on long sticks. They are honeybee magnets. Blooms are compact, about 0.25 inch across, and comprised of many miniature flowers. Blooms can grow in clusters that exceed 6 inches. The individual flowers are tiny and some shade of off-white, pastel pink, or hot-red pink. These bloom between April and September.

SEED: Flower heads turn into rust-colored seed heads. These seeds are adapted to take flight on the wind and are tiny and triangular and most have wings. They are golden brown to black and bulge in the middle. As the seeds are found above the plant and are abundant, this is an easy seed to harvest.

SEASON: Late summer through early winter

BENEFITS: Buckwheat has been eaten for millennia. Despite its name, buckwheat isn't actually a grain, and it is gluten free.

OTHER NAMES: None

chamise   rosemary

COMPARABLE SPECIES: There are two plants that might be confused with buckwheat: chamise and rosemary. Chamise (*Adenostoma fasciculatum*) grows in many of the same areas and has a similar structure and leaf. However, chamise's yellow-white flower stalks are arranged in sprays, not balls on sticks. Chamise is not edible. Rosemary (*Rosmarinus officinalis*) leaves are similar, but they grow alternate of each other, not in bunches. Rosemary's flowers are blue, and its flowers and leaves have been used as a cooking herb for millennia.

NOTES: Seeds are either ground into flour or boiled and made into mush. Remove as much debris, stems, and chaff as you can. Grinding up chaff will not hurt you. Leaves are edible after cooking, but you'd have to be hungry, as they aren't very tasty.

ELM, CHINESE
(Ulmus parvifolia)

WILD ORNAMENTAL

TYPE: Semi-deciduous to deciduous tree
STATUS: Non-native
LEAF ARRANGEMENT: Alternate and simple and oval with teeth
HARVEST TIME: September through October

HABITAT: A graceful ornamental tree common in urban areas, this tree is a weed along the coast and near-coastal waterways. It can be found in residential gardens and along city streets in communities along the coast and those in the mountains or deserts. It tolerates air pollution and compacted soils well.

GROWTH: Up to 50 feet tall and 60 feet wide, this is a graceful, big, spreading canopy tree. It has delicate-looking leaves. The trunks of the mature trees set it apart: dirty-gray outer bark flakes away to expose a smooth gray, green, orange, and yellow inner bark.

LEAVES: Growing alternate of each other along branches, the leaves are lance-like or ovate and up to 2.5 inches long. Leaf edges are distinctly serrated. In spring, the leaf color is a luxurious green; in fall it ranges from dirty-yellow to scarlet.

FLOWERS: Wind-pollinated, flowers are small, green, or red and bloom along branches and stems in small groups. They are easy to overlook. Chinese elm blooms August–September.

SEED: Adapted to take flight on the wind, seedpods are nearly round and encased in a small papery wing (achene) no bigger than 0.5 inch across. This type of seedpod is called a samara. The samara color changes from a transparent green to yellow-white to a parched reddish tan when mature.

SEASON: Samaras become edible late summer through early fall.

BENEFITS: Samaras contain significant amounts of protein and sugars, along with many nutrients.

OTHER NAMES: Lacebark elm

American elm   English elm   Siberian elm

COMPARABLE SPECIES: The only comparable species are the other *Ulmus* growing wildly or intentionally planted. These include the American elm (*U. americana*), English elm (*U. minor*), and Siberian elm (*U. pumila*). All three are just as edible.

NOTES: Green samaras are eaten raw or cooked. On older samaras, the flaky wing is removed and seeds are eaten raw or cooked. Young leaves can be eaten raw, but older ones should be cooked. The inner bark is also edible.

LOCUST, HONEY
(Gleditsia triacanthos)

ORNAMENTAL

TYPE: Deciduous tree
STATUS: Non-native
LEAF ARRANGEMENT: Alternate and bipinnately compound leaves
HARVEST TIME: Late summer through fall

HABITAT: An ornamental tree that was once widely planted in inland areas and desert communities, honey locust struggles in mild coastal climates. It is tough, surviving on a boulevard as easily as it does on a lawn. A native to the central and eastern U.S., it has been known to naturalize in areas but not with any great success.

GROWTH: Honey locust is stately and can grow up to 75 feet tall and 35 feet wide. Its bark is dark reddish brown with peeling fissures. Its distinguishing attributes are its finely divided leaves and long thorns.

LEAVES: Up to 10 inches long and resembling ferns, honey locust leaves are actually comprised of a mass of smaller leaflets (bipinnately compound). Leaflets are 0.75 to 1.5 inches long and oval. They are grass green to forest green in spring and golden yellow in fall.

FLOWERS: These dangling oblong blossoms don't look spectacular from a distance, but up close they are loaded with tiny, creamy green or yellow-white flowers. With their sweet fragrance, small pollinators love them. They bloom May–June.

SEEDPODS: Lengthy, slim, and twisted, seedpods can grow up to 18 inches long; when young, they are lime green. When mature, they are orange-brown, purplish brown, or a rich dark brown.

SEEDS: Seeds are pea-size, oval, and hard. Each seed is about 0.25 inch long and a golden to coffee-bean brown.

SEASON: Seedpods begin to ripen in mid- to late summer and remain harvestable well into fall.

BENEFITS: Both the seedpods and seeds have been eaten by humans and other animals for millennia. Seeds are high in protein, sugars, and many essential minerals. The sweet pulp is used for all kinds of delectable creations.

OTHER NAMES: Thorny locust

COMPARABLE SPECIES: The only other tree with thorns, twisting seedpods, and fern-like leaves is also from the pea family: the mesquite (page 134). Black locust is far larger than mesquite and its seedpods are almost twice as long.

NOTES: Immature seeds can be eaten raw, but mature ones should be boiled or roasted. Young seedpods have sweet pulp, while older pods are more bitter.

OAK
(Quercus spp.)

WILD ORNAMENTAL

TYPE: Evergreen or deciduous shrub or tree
STATUS: Most species are native
LEAF ARRANGEMENT: Alternate, simple, and toothed
or lobed
HARVEST TIME: Fall through winter

HABITAT: There are about 38 varieties of oak growing in Southern California. A majority of them are native. Oak can be found almost anywhere that gets more than 8 inches of rainfall per year. Coast live oak (*Q. agrifolia*) is possibly the most well-known and loved oak species in Southern California.

GROWTH: From massive and majestic trees to bristly shrubs, there is incredible variation among oaks. Acorns are their most distinguishing characteristic.

LEAVES: Oak leaves are thick and tough, but that is the only common characteristic among all species. Leaf size, edges, and color vary greatly between species. Some have holly-like leaves, some have smooth and oval leaves, and some have the classic curves and lobes of oak leaves found in the eastern U.S.

FLOWERS: Wind-pollinated, oak flowers are tiny and generally hang in long dangling sprays. They mostly bloom February–June.

SEED: Acorns are a distinctive feature. A majority have a scaly cap and a polished tan, tough outer shell.

SEASON: Acorns mature between fall and winter.

BENEFITS: Acorns have been eaten for millennia and are high in carbohydrates, fats, and protein.

OTHER NAMES: All oaks have a common first name, including black, blue, canyon live, coast live, desert, Engelmann, holly, interior, scrub, and valley.

COMPARABLE SPECIES: Only oaks produce acorns in Southern California.

NOTES: All acorns are edible and are processed to make flour. Unfortunately, acorns have bitter chemicals called tannins that must be leached before eating. There are many ways to leach out tannins to create edible flour. Here is one: Gather undamaged acorns. Remove the cap and hard outer shell by pounding or squeezing. Discard acorns with discolored or mushy (rotten) meat, acorns with damage, such as weevils, and last year's acorns, which are likely rotten. Boil acorns in at least three changes of water until the water stops becoming colored (or nearly so). This boiling process can take up to an hour. Dry the acorns in the sun or in an oven. Pound or grind acorns to make flour. Acorn flour is used in dishes (such as soups) or mixed with other flours to make breads.

SAGEBRUSH, BIG
(Artemisia tridentata)

WILD

TYPE: Shrub, summer deciduous
STATUS: Native
LEAF ARRANGEMENT: Alternate and simple
HARVEST TIME: Fall

HABITAT: This is a durable and dominant plant in the high desert. It is common on the eastern sides of the Sierra Nevada, our coastal mountains, and the San Bernardino Mountains, as well as in and around Cleveland National Forest. It can be found at elevations of up to 10,000 feet. It is uncommon in the lower deserts (it needs 10 inches of rainfall per year) and along the coast, where it is too humid.

GROWTH: Sagebrush is an erect shrub with many branches reaching for the sky. Although it can exceed 10 feet in height in summer-moist areas, big sagebrush is typically 3–6 feet tall and wide. Its trunk and older branches are thick and rough, with strips of grayish bark. Its most defining feature is its slim, wooly, highly aromatic leaf, which smells like turpentine.

LEAVES: Looking like an extended duck's foot, the leaves are thin and wedge-shaped with three lobes (toes) at the ends. They are 0.75–1.5

inches long and rarely wider than 0.5 inch. The leaves have a strong, musty turpentine smell and are a rich gray-green and hairy.

FLOWERS: Wind-pollinated and not dramatic, small flowers burst from spikes that radiate off branches. They are tubular and gold, yellow, and white. The flowers bloom July–August.

SEED: Seeds are tiny, oval, and straw-brown to black. They are less than 0.10 inch long.

SEASON: Seeds are ripe and harvestable in fall.

BENEFITS: American Indians throughout the West have eaten sagebrush for millennia.

OTHER NAMES: Mountain sagebrush and Great Basin sagebrush

California sagebrush

COMPARABLE SPECIES: The only other plant with linear gray leaves that smell like turpentine is the California sagebrush (*A. californica*). Luckily it has all the same qualities and is edible, but its seeds are harder to collect.

NOTES: Seeds are dried (naturally or roasted) and pounded into flour. The flour can either be eaten raw or used to make other dishes, like breads and soups.

WALNUT, SOUTHERN CALIFORNIA BLACK
(Juglans californica)

WILD

TYPE: Deciduous tree
STATUS: Native
LEAF ARRANGEMENT: Alternate and odd-pinnate
HARVEST TIME: Summer through fall

HABITAT: Needing more than 12 inches of rainfall per year, black walnut is common within 100 miles of the coast. It is often found on west-facing foothills. This native species can be found in the desert, but only along creeks and streams. It is not often found at elevations above 3,500 feet.

GROWTH: This endemic tree grows up to 30 feet tall and often wider. It is open and multi-branched. The bark is dirty gray-brown and greatly fissured. Few plants are found under black walnut because of the chemicals it produces that prevent other plants from growing. These powerful chemicals are found throughout the plant, but especially in the fruit's skin. (These compounds can even stain concrete!) The black walnut's ball-like fruit is its most distinguishing characteristic.

LEAVES: Walnut leaves can be more than 20 inches long, but they are comprised of up to 15 leaflets. Each leaflet is lance-shaped or elliptical and no longer than 3.5 inches. Leaf color is rich green in late winter through spring, yellow-green by late summer, and pumpkin red and scarlet yellow in fall. Leaves have a distinct sweet smell that is too much for some people.

FLOWERS: Male walnut flowers cascade forth in catkins from interior branches. Female flowers are small, singular, and found near the ends of branches. The tree is wind-pollinated and individual flowers are tiny and light green to muted yellow. It blooms May–June.

FRUIT: Ball-like and yellow-green when young and flaky, and black when mature, the fruit is about 1.25 inches in diameter. The skin of old fruit will stain your fingers. It is best to wear gloves.

SEED: A tough thick shell protects the nut. Although diminutive, the nut inside is hearty and tasty.

SEASON: Fruit ripens late summer through fall.

BENEFITS: The biggest benefit of walnuts is the oils. They produce omega-3 fatty acids, which are great for your heart. Walnuts also are high in calories, vitamin E, and loaded with antioxidant and anti-inflammatory properties.

OTHER NAMES: Southern black walnut

COMPARABLE SPECIES: Black walnut's ball-like yellow-green fruit is unique.

NOTES: Kernels are eaten raw or cooked. Remove the hull, clean the nut, dry it in the sun or in the oven for 12 hours at its lowest temperature, and crack the nut with a vice to get to the meat.

Other Plants with Edible Seeds

Agave *Agave* spp. (page 148)

Bulrush *Bolboschoenus* spp. and *Schoenoplectus* spp. (page 212)

Carob *Ceratonia siliqua* (page 126)

Cattail *Typha* spp. (page 42)

Cheeseweed *Malva parviflora* (page 44)

Chickweed *Stellaria media* (page 66)

Clover *Trifolium* spp. (page 152)

Currant and gooseberry *Ribes* spp. (page 100)

Fennel, sweet *Foeniculum vulgare* (page 48)

Lambsquarters and goosefoot *Chenopodium album* and *C. murale* (page 52)

Locust, black *Robinia pseudoacacia* (page 158)

Mallow *Malva* spp. (page 132)

Mesquite *Prosopis* spp. (page 134)

Mustard *Brassica* spp. (page 54)

Nut grass (yellow and purple) and papyrus *Cyperus esculentus, C. rotundus,* and *C. papyrus* (page 198)

Plantain, common *Plantago major* (page 76)

Radish, wild *Raphanus sativus* (page 60)

Saltbush, big *Atriplex lentiformis* (page 84)

Shepherd's purse *Capsella bursa-pastoris* (page 200)

Yucca *Yucca* spp. (page 142)

Watercress *Nasturtium officinale* (page 220)

BUCKWHEAT

BULL THISTLE

ROOTS

High in starch and many minerals and nutrients, roots have long been considered a famine food, but that does not have to be the case. Roots add density, texture, and flavor to salads, stews, and stir-fries.

IMPORTANT: Only harvest roots from areas where you know the soil isn't contaminated. Root crops readily absorb metals and toxins from the environment.

CHICORY
(*Cichorium intybus*)

WILD

TYPE: Perennial
STATUS: Non-native
LEAF ARRANGEMENT: Basal when young; sheathed and opposite when found on a stem
HARVEST TIME: Summer through fall

HABITAT: Found from Santa Barbara to San Diego and up to 75 miles inland, this perennial isn't always common, but it can be found. It tolerates dry conditions but needs winter moisture and well-drained soils. It lives close to people, especially our roads, trails, and rocky disturbances. It is not likely to be in remote areas.

GROWTH: A fleshy mass when young and a tall spindly weed when mature, chicory is hard to identify unless it's blooming. It grows 2–6 feet tall and 1–3 feet wide. Stems are stout, hollow, and have bristles. Like its relatives, the dandelion and sow thistle, chicory has milky sap.

LEAVES: Leaves growing from the base are 4–8 inches long and generally oblong, but their shape varies greatly. Some are severely pinnately lobed (or toothed), while others look more like a paddle. Leaves on the stem and higher up are linear, smaller (1–3 inches long), and have smooth edges or are lightly toothed. Leaf color ranges from grass green to rich forest green.

FLOWERS: This beauty is in the aster/sunflower family, and it absolutely looks like it. Pale sky-blue rays 1 inch in diameter bloom in clusters of up to 5. The tiny petals have a notch and are slightly serrated. Flowers are sometimes white. It blooms May through August.

SEASON: Roots are better when they are mature and full of stored energy; July through early November is best. The leaves are bitter and best eaten when young; harvest January through May.

BENEFITS: Roots are packed with starchy energy and have some sugar and protein. Leaves provide energy and iron, as well as vitamins B, C, and K. They also contain antioxidants.

OTHER NAMES: Blue dandelion, coffee weed

dandelion   hedge mustard   sheep sorrel   shepherd's purse   sow thistle

COMPARABLE SPECIES: Luckily, all the plants resembling this perennial are edible. When chicory is young, it looks like dandelion, hedge mustard, sheep sorrel, shepherd's purse, and sow thistle.

NOTES: The root is boiled, sautéed, or roasted. It is a great source of energy. Younger roots are more palatable than old ones. Roasted and ground roots are used as a caffeine-free substitute for coffee. The leaves are eaten raw or cooked, but they taste better before the plant flowers. All leaves are bitter, and much of the bitterness can be cooked, boiled, or steamed out.

Purple Nut Grass

Papyrus

NUT GRASS (YELLOW AND PURPLE) AND PAPYRUS
(Cyperus esculentus, C. rotundus, and C. papyrus)

WILD

TYPE: Perennial herb and a grass-like sedge
STATUS: Native and non-native
LEAF ARRANGEMENT: Grass-like
HARVEST TIME: Anytime, but late spring is best

HABITAT: Nut grass and papyrus are common in urban areas and are found in gardens and landscapes that are too moist and too shady. They tolerate salts well and can be found around agriculture too. Only yellow nut grass (*C. esculentus*) is native.

GROWTH: Yellow and purple nut grass look much like perennial grasses, but their leaves are stout and erect, not floppy. Nut grass's most distinguishing trait is its triangular stem. While nut grass can grow to 20 inches tall, it is generally shorter. Papyrus is much larger and its stout, narrow leaves grow 4–8 feet tall and are topped with a tuft of grass-like slim blades that reach 10 inches long. Nearly every part of these plants is green. All three are aggressive spreaders.

FLOWERS: Wind-pollinated, the flowers are not showy, but the flower stalk and arrangement make the entire ensemble unique. Flower spikes look like fireworks exploding above the plant; umbrella-like structures branch out with many tiny light-green to hay-colored flowers.

ROOTS: The yellow and purple nut grasses produce edible tubers; papyrus nut grass produces edible rhizomes. Tubers are roughly round and about 0.33 inch in diameter. Immediately below papyrus's crown, and buried underneath a mass of fine roots, is the rhizome, which grows up to 12 inches long and up to 2.5 inches in diameter.

SEASON: These roots are harvested year-round, although late spring may produce the sweetest.

BENEFITS: Nut grass and papyrus have been eaten for centuries.

OTHER NAMES: Nut sedge, flat grass, chufa

COMPARABLE SPECIES: Sedges have edges, which separate them from grasses, which have a hollow stem, and rushes, which have a round stem. Nut grass is the most pervasive sedge in urban landscapes. As a rule, sedges have edible roots.

NOTES: Peeled rhizomes and tubers can be eaten raw or steamed, but they are best roasted, from which they are either eaten alone, added to dishes, or ground to make flour. Roasted tubers are earthy, a little sweet, and tasty. Dried seeds are also edible.

ROOTS

SHEPHERD'S PURSE
(Capsella bursa-pastoris)

WILD

TYPE: Annual

STATUS: Non-native

LEAF ARRANGEMENT: Basal, with pinnately and deeply
lobed leaves

HARVEST TIME: Any time of year, but late spring is best

HABITAT: This plant is a people-follower and is found on the islands,
right along the coast, and into the mountains and down their eastern
sides, but it is not as prevalent in the desert, except in the mountains.
It prefers disturbed, slightly acidic, and moderately deep soils.

GROWTH: This fleshy, erect-stemmed annual grows between 4 inches and
2.5 feet tall and 6–9 inches wide. The whole plant is pale to moderately
deep green. This widespread annual is a member of the mustard family.

LEAVES: Young leaves grow from the crown (basal growth) on small stems
in an oblong shape, and they are slightly hairy, pinnate, and deeply
lobed with a paddle-like end. They are no more than 6 inches long and
1.5 inches wide, with smooth edges. Older leaves on the flowering stalk

are alternate, lance-like, have toothed edges, and are about 3 inches long and 0.5 inch wide. Leaves are typically a pale green to grass green.

FLOWERS: Short-lived flowers cluster at the end of erect stalks (raceme). No more than 0.12 inch wide, they have 4 small, pale-white petals. These stalks grow up to 2 feet tall, but most are shorter. It blooms throughout the year.

SEEDPODS: The plant is famous for its odd-looking fruits, which resemble a tiny shepherd's purse. They are triangular or heart-shaped, flat, and about 0.25 inch long.

SEASON: Late spring is best for roots. Winter and spring are best for greens. And spring and summer are the best seasons for the seeds.

BENEFITS: Roots are high in starch. Leaves are rich in calcium, iron, phosphorus, potassium, some protein, and sodium, as well as vitamins A, C, and K, making this plant almost a superfood. It possesses anti-inflammatory properties that are reputedly great for stiff joints.

OTHER NAMES: None

chicory   dandelion   hedge mustard   sheep sorrel

COMPARABLE SPECIES: Luckily, all the plants that look like shepherd's purse are edible. These plants include chicory (page 196), dandelion (page 46), mustard (page 54), and sheep sorrel (page 86).

NOTES: These roots are small, and you will need to dig up several plants for a meal. They are cleaned and either diced and added to dishes or dried/roasted and ground up for use in soups. Young leaves and flower stalks are eaten raw or cooked. The taste is mildly peppery. Older leaves are far too peppery for consumption. Seeds are also used as a seasoning.

SOURGRASS
(Oxalis pes-caprae)

WILD

TYPE: Perennial
STATUS: Non-native
LEAF ARRANGEMENT: Basal rosette
HARVEST TIME: Leaves year-round; flowers winter
through summer

HABITAT: Sourgrass is a people-follower and prefers acidic, fertile, and slightly compacted soils. It does not tolerate a deep frost, which means this perennial is sparse in areas without a coastal influence. They are more likely found in areas with filtered shade than in full sun or deep shade.

GROWTH: Fleshy, delicate, and a voracious spreader, sourgrass is easy to find in and around urban features. The plant grows to about 6 inches high and can get up to 1 foot wide. It spreads by underground tubers and seed.

LEAVES: Each leaf is comprised of 3 leaflets, each of which are heart-shaped and join to the stem at the heart's point. The leaf sits atop a long thin stem (petiole) that rises above the plant, sometimes as tall as 1 foot. Leaves are generally a pale green and may be spotted.

FLOWERS: Flowers rise above the plant on thin, swaying stems. The flower is a pale buttercup-yellow and has 5 petals. Sourgrass blooms December–June.

ROOTS: The small tubers are the edible portions of the root. They are ball-like and rarely larger than 0.5 inch in diameter.

SEASON: Winter through early summer are the best times for leaves and flowers, but this plant can be eaten anytime it is found, which makes it a year-round harvest in many parts of Southern California.

BENEFITS: Sourgrass is high in vitamin C and also contains vitamin A. It is high in oxalic acid, which tastes sour (and is toxic in high doses), and it is best if mixed with the more alkaline greens, such as mustard and purslane. This plant is great at quenching thirst and adds a lemony punch to salads and drinks.

OTHER NAMES: Bermuda buttercup, common yellow oxalis, common yellow woodsorrel, lemon clover

clover   black medick

COMPARABLE SPECIES: Clover (*Trifolium* spp., page 152) is the closest plant that resembles sourgrass, and luckily, it is edible. Black medick (*Medicago lupulina*, page 176) is also similar. The leaves and seeds of black medick are edible, but they should be cooked first. Although black medick has the familiar trefoil and oval leaflets, it grows taller, has stouter stems, and the flower head is comprised of many tubular mustard-yellow flowers.

NOTES: Roots can be eaten raw, but they taste better if boiled or cooked first. They have a nutty, sweet flavor. Leaves, stems, and flowers are edible. The leaves have a lemony, acidic flavor. The acidic nature might be too much for some people. All *Oxalis* species are edible.

SWORD FERN
(*Nephrolepis spp.* and *Polystichum spp.*)

WILD ORNAMENTAL

TYPE: Rhizomatous fern (a fern that spreads by a rhizome)
STATUS: Native and non-native
LEAF ARRANGEMENT: Basal grower, odd-pinnate leaf
HARVEST TIME: Spring

HABITAT: In the wild, sword ferns grow in shady moist canyons and crevices. They might also be found in the crotch of a tree or in the cracks of boulders. In urban areas, they grow on the north and eastern sides of homes and buildings. They are also a common indoor plant. The non-native southern sword fern (*Nephrolepis cordifolia*) is the one with delicious tubers. The plant is commercially sold, easy to find, and is a weed along the coast. The native varieties (*Polystichum* spp.) have small, edible rhizomes and are more likely found in the foothills.

GROWTH: Few common names are as direct—each frond looks like a sword jutting out from a bulbous mass that looks like a hilt. Sword fern height varies between 1 and 4 feet tall. They spread by underground roots (rhizomes), and some varieties can overwhelm moist, shady areas.

LEAVES: Fronds are long, narrow, and light green to rich green. They are comprised of many small, leathery sword-shaped leaflets, each with toothed edges. The leaflets of *Nephrolepis* slightly overlap each other at the base; there is a small gap between *Polystichum* leaflets.

FLOWERS: Sword ferns produce spores on the underside of their fronds.

ROOTS: The tubers are marble-size and creamy tan when cleaned. Rhizomes are rarely larger than 0.25 inch in diameter, but they can be up to 6 inches long. They are a creamy yellow after peeling.

SEASON: Rhizomes and tubers will be plumpest in spring.

BENEFITS: Tubers mostly consist of water and carbohydrates, but they do contain some protein and nutrients. The rhizomes were eaten as famine food by indigenous peoples in California and are mostly starch.

OTHER NAMES: Southern sword fern, western swordfern, Boston swordfern

COMPARABLE SPECIES: There are two native ferns that are sometimes confused with sword fern. The male fern (*Dryopteris filix-mas*) is similar, but its fronds are far broader, not as erect, and the leaflets more deeply cut. The giant chain fern (*Woodwardia fimbriata*) is also similar, but it often grows much taller and its fronds are much broader.

NOTES: Treat them just like potatoes. Rhizomes and tubers are eaten raw, boiled, or roasted. Tubers are refreshing (they are mostly water) and rhizomes are small and bland. If you're trying to protect the fern, dig it up, cut away the desired parts, and replant it.

BULL THISTLE
(Cirsium vulgare)

WILD

TYPE: Perennial herb
STATUS: Non-native
LEAF ARRANGEMENT: Basal with central flower stalk
HARVEST TIME: Anytime, but spring is best

HABITAT: Fairly common within 120 miles of the coast and can be found at elevations of up to 8,000 feet. While rare in the desert, it can be found along agricultural waterways. It has a strong tolerance for salty soils. Look for bull thistle on disturbed land, near agriculture, and in areas that have been grazed.

GROWTH: Bull thistle looks like a smaller, greener, and more lethal artichoke (the plants are related). The vegetative mass typically grows to 1.5 feet tall, and the flower stalk can reach more than 6 feet tall. Its long spines and spined leaves distinguish the bull thistle from other thistles.

LEAVES: The leaves can be short, slim, and slightly lobed, or long and deeply lobed. The edges of all leaves have painfully sharp spines. Leaf length varies between 4 and 16 inches. Leaf color ranges from grass green to blue green and gray blue green.

FLOWERS: Bull thistle flower stalks are tall and gangly and branch out in all directions with many small artichoke-like flowers. The bulb-like flower is no more than 1.5 inches wide and up to 2 inches tall. The top quarter is an eruption of lilac- or purple-colored hair; the bottom three-quarters is a mass of spines. It blooms June–September.

ROOTS: The roots are long and meaty. The edible portions can be as deep as 1 foot under the surface, and most grow straight down, meaning a lot of digging is required to get at it.

SEASON: Roots can be dug up anytime of the year, but they are best just after the spring.

BENEFITS: The thistles have been keeping desperate pioneers alive for hundreds of years. Whether it's the leaves and roots, the fleshy stalks, or flower heads, every thistle has something to provide.

OTHER NAMES: No other names

COMPARABLE SPECIES: With its spiny leaves and distinct flower head, the only things that resemble bull thistle are the other thistle species.

NOTES: Roots are dug up, washed, boiled for 20 minutes, and then sautéed with butter and spices. Flower stalks are edible and should be treated like the root. The leaves and flower are also edible after cooking.

Other Plants with Edible Roots

Bulrush *Bolboschoenus* spp. and *Schoenoplectus* spp. (page 212)

Cattail *Typha* spp. (page 42)

Dandelion *Taraxacum* spp. (page 46)

Filaree, red-stemmed *Erodium cicutarium* (page 50)

Radish, wild *Raphanus sativus* (page 60)

Sow thistle *Sonchus* spp. (page 88)

Speedwell, water *Veronica anagallis-aquatica* (page 218)

Thistle, milk *Silybum marianum* (page 168)

PAPYRUS

WRACK

POISONOUS PLANTS

Whether through misidentification or a misstep, failing to recognize poisonous plants can ruin your day, and in the worst case, even cost you your life. The first step in successful foraging is being able to identify the poisonous plants that follow. The goal is to become competent enough to share your knowledge.

CASTOR BEAN
(Ricinus communis)

WILD

TYPE: Perennial/shrub
STATUS: Non-native
LEAF ARRANGEMENT: Alternate and palmate
POISONOUS PARTS: The whole plant, but particularly the seeds

HABITAT: This plant is a people-follower that does not like a freeze. It is very common everywhere west of Joshua Tree National Park, especially in areas with direct coastal influence. It can tolerate drought as well as salty and compacted soils. It can be found along roads, on commercial properties, and in our state parks.

GROWTH: This shrub can sometimes look like a small tree and grows 3–12 feet tall and often as wide. It grows upright, and its burgundy/brown stems and huge green leaves are its two distinguishing attributes.

LEAVES: When compared to most wild plants, the castor bean's leaves are huge: generally 1–2 feet in diameter, and sometimes to 3 feet. They are round but have 5–11 severely toothed lobes. New leaves are shiny burgundy to reddish green; mature leaves are a glossy grass green. Even at a distance, the big leaves make this plant easy to identify.

FLOWERS: Castor bean flowers are small and bloom in dense clusters along flower stalks that are 3–12 inches long. Male flowers occupy the lower part of the stalk and are yellow-green and cup-shaped. Female flowers, although fewer in number, sit above the males and have distinct red hairs (stigmas) erupting from the center. Although it most often flowers in summer, it is an intermittent bloomer and can flower throughout the year.

FRUIT: These distinct fruit are a Ping-Pong ball shape, a blazing pinkish red, and adorned with fleshy bendable spikes. They are between 0.6 and 0.75 inch in diameter. When immature, they are bluish light green.

OTHER NAMES: Castor oil plant.

Japanese aralia

COMPARABLE SPECIES: Only Japanese aralia (*Fatsia japonica*) resembles castor bean, although this is strictly an ornamental plant and cannot be found in the wild. The young leaves and shoots of *Fatsia* are edible (they are cooked or steamed).

NOTES: You will get sick if you eat any part of Castor Bean. Its seeds are its most toxic part.

IVY
(Hedera spp.)

WILD

TYPE: Vine
STATUS: Non-native
LEAF ARRANGEMENT: Alternate, simple, and with 3–5 lobes
POISONOUS PARTS: Leaves and berries (do not eat or handle)

HABITAT: Two varieties of ivy are common: Algerian (*Hedera canariensis*) and English (*Hedera helix*). Ivy is both a weed in areas within 100 miles of the coast and a common ground cover grown throughout Southern California. It flourishes alongside development and makes the best of salty or compact soils. It prefers slightly acidic soils.

GROWTH: Ivy's soft and supple branches have nodes that can either grow sticky feet and climb walls or trees, or grow roots and start new plants. Ivy is aggressive and can be found climbing up telephone poles and covering large urban properties. Ivy's distinguishing characteristic is its moderately large and mostly glossy dark green leaves.

LEAVES: Ivy plants have two types of leaves: juvenile and mature. Juvenile leaves have 3–5 lobes and some, like needlepoint ivy, are deeply lobed. Mature leaves are heart-shaped or oval with a pronounced point. Both types of leaves range 2–6 inches long and 1–5 inches wide. All leaves are thick, glossy, mostly rich green, and have smooth edges and surfaces.

FLOWERS: Ivy produces ball-like clusters of tiny flowers that are green to yellow white. They bloom April through June. The round bluish black berries that follow persist all summer.

OTHER NAMES: Algerian ivy, English ivy, needlepoint ivy

blackberry   wild grape   currant   gooseberry

COMPARABLE SPECIES: There are three plants that might be mistaken for ivy: blackberry (page 98), grape (page 104), and plants in the genus *Ribes* (page 100), which include currants and gooseberries. All can be found growing in the same locations. Blackberry has a similar-looking leaf, but it is hairy, and its branches and stems have thorns. Wild grape's leaf is similar in shape, but it has toothed edges and a fuzzy texture. Some *Ribes* species (such as currant and gooseberry) produce similarly shaped leaves, but their texture is rough and the edges are toothed.

NOTES: Every part of this plant is toxic to humans. Do not eat any part of it, and avoid getting the sap on your skin, as it can cause irritation, itching, and rashes.

JIMSONWEED
(Datura spp.*)*

WILD

TYPE: Annual and perennial
STATUS: Four species are native, with one non-native
species present
LEAF ARRANGEMENT: Alternate and simple
POISONOUS PARTS: Every part

HABITAT: Five *Datura* species are found in Southern California. They are common throughout the region, although rare in the low desert. By far the most common species is the native *Datura wrightii* (*D. meteloides*). A close relative, *Brugmansia* (angel's trumpet), is an ornamental genus and regularly planted in urban landscapes—and it too has *Datura's* toxic properties.

GROWTH: Wild *Datura* grows to 3 feet tall and more than 6 feet wide. It can be a large dense mass of leaves or a shrub with trailing tentacles that looks vine-like. Its large, dangling, trumpet-like flower is its most distinguishing attribute.

LEAVES: Arrowhead in shape, 3–8 inches long, and irregularly lobed, the leaf has distinct indented veins and a bluish green color. The leaves are also thick and have an unpleasant odor.

FLOWERS: Jimsonweed produces large, trumpet-like flowers; the bright white flowers open at night and are pollinated by nocturnal creatures, such as bats and moths. Sweetly fragrant in the evening, they may wither during the day. *D. wrightii* blooms February to October, but most other varieties bloom during summer.

OTHER NAMES: Desert thorn apple, sacred Datura, pricklyburr

wild cucumber   coyote melon   buffalo gourd

COMPARABLE SPECIES: The arrow-like leaves and trumpet-like flowers set *Datura* apart from any edible plant. However, *Datura* is often confused with other, much less toxic plants, such as wild cucumber (*Marah* spp.), coyote melon (*Cucurbita palmate*), and buffalo gourd (*Cucurbita foetidissima*).

NOTES: Getting sap from this plant in your eyes leads to irritation, dilated pupils, and blurry vision. Eating any part of the plant leads to nausea, increased heart rate, and maybe delirium. An extract from this plant makes a dangerous narcotic.

LUPINE
(Lupinus spp.)

TYPE: Annual, perennial, subshrub, and shrub
STATUS: Native and non-native
LEAF ARRANGEMENT: Mostly alternate (some opposite) and compound palmate
POISONOUS PARTS: All parts, but seedpods and seeds the most

WILD

HABITAT: Lupine can be found throughout the state, including at some of our highest and lowest elevations. It is a member of the pea family and tolerates an incredible range of soils. Annual lupine species are abundant following above-average winter rainfall.

GROWTH: There are more than 100 species of lupine growing in California. They range from small, fleshy plants to brittle specimens reaching 8 feet tall. Luckily, lupine's leaves and flowers make it distinguishable.

LEAVES: One leaf is comprised of many narrow leaflets that radiate from a central stem (petiole), looking something like an exploding star. Typically, there are between 5 and 12 leaflets and the entire leaf is 0.5–3 inches wide. Leaf color ranges between a light grass green, a rich blue green, and a polished steel gray.

FLOWERS: Lupine is prized for its flowers. They produce tall flower spikes that erupt with a mass of pea-like flowers, all with the lupine's classic pouting lower lip. Color varies between species and includes blue, lavender, pink, purple, violet, white, and yellow.

SEEDPOD: Resembling a bean pod, lupine's seedpods look edible from a distance. Up close, their hairy or velvety nature sets them apart. Pods are erect (not drooping), flattish, and 0.5–2 inches long. Each pod contains 2–11 seeds.

OTHER NAMES: No other names

COMPARABLE SPECIES: There are no comparable species.

NOTES: As a rule, foragers avoid lupine. Not all species are poisonous, but the benefits do not outweigh the risks. Poisonous lupine contains toxic alkaloids, which, if swallowed, can lead to stomach upset, nervousness, difficulty breathing, discomfort, and convulsions. Toxic varieties also cause birth defects in livestock. The two known varieties of poisonous lupine in Southern California are silvery lupine (*L. argenteus*) and summer lupine (*L. formosus*). Silvery lupine is rarely found in San Bernardino. Summer lupine is commonly found within 110 miles of the coast.

MISTLETOE
(Phoradendron spp.)

WILD

TYPE: Parasitic shrub
STATUS: Native
LEAF ARRANGEMENT: Opposite and simple
POISONOUS PARTS: All parts of this plant are poisonous; the berries and leaves are most toxic.

HABITAT: There are six species of native mistletoe growing in Southern California. This parasitic shrub can be found everywhere—from the coast to the mountains and from the low desert to the high desert. Spread by birds, this plant roots into trees and large shrubs and steals its host's nutrients and water. It is found in city parks and national forests alike.

GROWTH: This tree-dweller can grow to be a 3x3-foot mass of stems, small leaves, and berries. Mistletoe generally looks like some part of the host plant. It is rare to find this plant growing at eye level; it is usually in the upper branches of a tree.

LEAVES: Some mistletoe species have leaves that are tiny and scale-like; others are oval and just over 1 inch long and 0.75 inch wide. Leaf color ranges from greenish yellow and yellow-green to gray-green and grass green. Mistletoe species that are green and larger-leafed are semi-parasitic, producing some of their own resources.

FLOWERS: The flowers are tiny, yellow, and greenish, and borne en masse on small stalks (inflorescence). The flower is nearly inconspicuous. Each mistletoe blooms at a different time of year, and between all of the species, there is always a mistletoe blooming in Southern California.

FRUIT: The fruit resembles a gum ball, but much smaller; mistletoe produces an abundance of fruit. They are about 0.12 inch in diameter, round, and set on stems that grow to 2 inches long. The fruit's skin is smooth and colored cherry red, pink, or dull white.

OTHER NAMES: None, though each species has a qualifier, such as American mistletoe, California mistletoe, desert mistletoe, or mesquite mistletoe.

COMPARABLE SPECIES: There are no comparable species.

NOTES: Eating berries or leaves can lead to stomach upset and diarrhea. While there have been cases of children dying from ingesting berries, those cases are rare and involved many berries.

OLEANDER
(Nerium oleander)

WILD ORNAMENTAL

TYPE: Shrub

STATUS: Non-native

LEAF ARRANGEMENT: Opposite or in whorls of 3 and simple lance-like

POISONOUS PARTS: All parts are toxic to ingest, and some people develop skin problems from handling the plant.

HABITAT: Found all along the coast and all the way to our eastern border, this durable shrub is widely planted in Southern California. It is hardy and needs little care and water. You'll find it along freeways, around shopping centers, and in your neighbor's garden. It is also found growing naturally in the foothills.

GROWTH: Oleander is widely planted because it is long-lived, simple to maintain, and creates a tidy hedge. It grows densely, reaching 3–20 feet tall and 3–12 feet wide.

LEAVES: The leaves are narrow, 4–12 inches long, and thick, and leaf color ranges from a rich deep green to a yellowish green. Both the leaf texture and the edges are smooth. Crushed leaves have an unpleasant odor.

FLOWERS: Oleander flowers burst in clusters from the ends of branches and stems. They are slightly fragrant; 2–3 inches across; and come in many colors, including white, pink, red, and salmon.

OTHER NAMES: None

California bay

COMPARABLE SPECIES: California bay (*Umbellularia californica*) is the edible plant that oleander most resembles. Both have lance-like and glossy, rich green leaves. However, bay's leaves are highly and pleasantly scented, unlike oleander's. And bay does not have showy flowers, like oleander. Luckily, these two plants are rarely found growing together.

NOTES: This plant is both toxic to consume and handle. Ingesting just a little piece of a leaf can cause severe sickness—eating more can cause death. Many people cannot even touch it because it is a skin irritant and can lead to blisters, rashes, and/or swelling. Furthermore, burning the plant and inhaling the smoke is lethal.

Poison hemlock stem

POISON HEMLOCK
(Conium maculatum)

WILD

TYPE: Perennial
STATUS: Non-native
LEAF ARRANGEMENT: Opposite; 2–4 odd-pinnate triangle-shaped leaflets
POISONOUS PARTS: Eating any part of this plant can cause death.

HABITAT: This beautiful perennial is predominately found along the coast. It has a high tolerance for salty soil. A line drawn from Bakersfield to Hesperia to Mount Laguna represents its eastern boundary. It will not be found in the desert. The plant prefers natural areas and wet areas impacted by urban runoff.

GROWTH: Delicate looking but stout, this perennial grows to 2–8 feet tall and half as wide. Stems are hollow, hairless, and a light green and spotted or streaked with purple. Its robust size and fern-like leaves are its distinguishing characteristics.

LEAVES: Lacy and large, leaves can grow to 1½ feet long and 1 foot wide. They are triangular in overall shape. Each leaf is comprised of 3–13 leaflets (odd-pinnate) and each of these is lance-shaped, highly dissected, and looking frilly. Leaves have an unpleasant smell when crushed.

FLOWERS: The blossom is beautiful and looks like that of a carrot. Its wide umbrella-like shape (umbel) is comprised of many smaller umbels, which in turn consist of a mass of tiny flowers no larger than 0.1 inch wide. All of this creates the perfect landing pad for pollinators. It blooms April through September.

OTHER NAMES: Spotted hemlock

chervil   fennel   wild carrot   wild celery

COMPARABLE SPECIES: The four edible plants poison hemlock is most confused with are chervil (*Anthriscus* spp.), fennel (*Foeniculum vulgare*, page 48), wild carrot (*Daucus* spp.), and wild celery (*Apium graveolens*, page 214). Chervil is much smaller, and its leaves smell like anise. Fennel leaves are finely organized in linear divisions and not comprised of many smaller leaflets; fennel leaves are bluish green, not turf green, and it has yellow flowers, not white. Wild carrot only grows to 3 feet, not 8 feet; its leaves and stems are slightly bristly, not smooth, and its leaves are finer and the flower heads smaller. Wild celery has the familiar celery stalk and is not round or smooth; it only grows to 2–3 feet tall, not 8 feet; its leaves smell pleasant when crushed, not foul, and its flower heads are much smaller (but still white).

NOTES: All parts of this plant are poisonous. If ingested, poison hemlock causes nausea, vomiting, convulsions, and even death.

POISON OAK
(Rhus diversiloba)

WILD

TYPE: Deciduous vining shrub
STATUS: Native
LEAF ARRANGEMENT: Opposite and trifoliate
POISONOUS PARTS: All

HABITAT: Poison oak is widespread along the coast and up and down both sides of the coastal mountains. It is rarely found farther east than the San Bernardino Mountains. It needs moderate precipitation. Poison oak tolerates compacted soils and grows well next to human development. Canyons, college campuses, the cooler sides of dry hills, ravines, and vacant lots are just some of its many habitats.

GROWTH: This is a devil of a plant. It can be found in small solitary patches no more than 2 feet high or as a sprawling mass covering hundreds of square feet. It can form as a ground cover or as a vine that rises 30 feet into the branches of a tree. All of poison oak's stems and branches are spindly and rambling. Older branches tend to be gray-brown, whereas younger ones are reddish brown.

LEAVES: Leaves of three, let it be! Poison oak has a trifoliate leaf, which means it is 1 leaf comprised of 3 leaflets. The terminal leaflet (the one at the end) might get to 5 inches long and 3 inches wide. The two lateral leaflets get up to 3 inches long and 2.5 inches wide. The margins of each can be scalloped or lobed. Leaf stems are 0.5–4 inches long. Poison oak changes color with the seasons: shiny and bronze-hued in late winter, it is a glossy light green to forest green through midsummer and yellow-orange to blazing red in fall.

FLOWERS: Tiny, creamy white-green flowers dangle from pyramid-shaped clusters (inflorescence). These clusters range from 0.75 to 3 inches long. Individual flowers are less than 0.1 inch in diameter. It blooms March through June.

OTHER NAMES: None

blackberry   currant   gooseberry

COMPARABLE SPECIES: Blackberry and plants from the genus *Ribes* (which includes currant and gooseberry) could be mistaken for poison oak. For details on those plants, see page 98 and 100, respectively.

NOTES: Do not touch or eat poison oak, and never inhale the smoke from its burning wood. The entirety of the plant is highly toxic. Touching it can cause irritation, swelling, and intense itching that lasts up to two weeks. Consuming it or inhaling smoke from the burning wood can cause death. This common plant is tough to distinguish when it is leafless in winter; look for rambling stems that are mud brown with red hues.

Petty spurge

SPURGE AND GOPHER PLANT
(Euphorbia spp.)

WILD

TYPE: Annual or perennial
STATUS: Native and non-native
LEAF ARRANGEMENT: Varies with species
POISONOUS PARTS: The milky sap is a skin irritant; eating the plant will cause much discomfort.

HABITAT: There are more than 50 wild species of *Euphorbia* in California, with 20 species available at retail nurseries. Euphorbia is likely to be found in any area without a prolonged freeze.

GROWTH: The three varieties of most concern to foragers are the prostrate spurges, petty spurge, and the gopher plant. The prostrate spurges (*Euphorbia hypericifolia* and *Euphorbia maculata*) are low growing and mat forming, might have red stems, have small leaves, and only live a season or two. Petty spurge (*Euphorbia peplus*) is delicate looking and 2–12 inches tall with reddish stems. The gopher plant (*Euphorbia lathyris*) is erect and grows to 4 feet tall and 1 foot wide.

LEAVES: The leaves of prostrate spurge are never more than 0.75 inch long and 0.25 inch wide, and they are often spotted. Their color varies between light green, rich green, and brownish green. Leaves of petty spurge are oval, rarely more than 0.25 inch long and lime green. And the leaves of the gopher plant are up to 6 inches long, very narrow, and oppositely attached. Their color ranges from pale green to bluish green.

FLOWERS: Spurge blooms at the axis of stems and leaves and the flowers are nearly inconspicuous. They are cup-shaped, light white or pale red, and never more than 0.12 inch in diameter. Petty spurge has small, round flowers that are green or yellow. Gopher plant's flowers sit atop the foliage in clusters; they're almost translucent and pale green, yellow-green, and yellow.

OTHER NAMES: Prostrate varieties are also known as sandmat. Gopher plant is called caper spurge, compass plant, and mole plant.

purslane

chickweed

sow thistle

COMPARABLE SPECIES: The prostrate spurges look like purslane (page 80). Purslane does not have spurge's white milky sap. Petty spurge looks like chickweed (page 66), but it is typically taller and has translucent flowers and milky sap. And a young gopher plant might be confused with sow thistle (page 88). The difference is in the edges of their leaves: gopher plant's leaf edges are smooth and sow thistle's are ragged and toothed.

copper plant

poinsettia

sticks-on-fire

NOTES: All Euphorbias are poisonous; this includes the commonly planted copper plant (*Euphorbia cotinifolia*, a tree), poinsettia (*Euphorbia pulcherrima*), and sticks-on-fire (*Euphorbia tirucalli*). If any parts of these plants are ingested, expect nausea and vomiting. If you get its latex gooey sap on your skin, expect discomfort and irritation.

STINGING NETTLE

(Urtica spp.)

WILD

TYPE: Annual and perennial

STATUS: Native and non-native

LEAF ARRANGEMENT: Opposite with oblong and fiercely serrated margins

POISONOUS PARTS: The entire plant, but particularly the seeds

WARNING: If you brush against it with bare skin, the leaves will sting you, causing intense discomfort.

HABITAT: Any area that gets at least 11 inches of rain per year and is within 80 miles of the coast could be home to stinging nettle. It thrives near human development. It is also found along the ocean, at elevations of up to 8,000 feet, as well as on the eastern side of the more coastal mountains. It peters out in the low desert. It is more likely found under trees than in full sun.

GROWTH: An erect branching annual or perennial; nettles become somewhat woody. They range in height from 4 inches to 2 feet and have single- or multi-branched stems.

LEAVES: Nettle leaves are distinctly oblong or spear-like; the edges are uniquely serrated, resembling piranha teeth. Each leaf is 0.75–2 inches long, attached with small stems, and found opposite another leaf. Leaf color ranges from pale green to forest green.

FLOWERS: Tiny wind-pollinated flowers form on small wispy stems from the axis of the leaves and stalks. They range in color from green to brown. Varieties in coastal areas bloom January–April; in the mountains, they bloom May–September.

OTHER NAMES: Nettle.

western nettle   hairy beggarticks   trailing mallow   coyote mint   lemon balm

COMPARABLE SPECIES: The leaves of stinging nettle resemble many edible plants, including western nettle (*Hesperocnide tenella*), hairy beggarticks (*Bidens pilosa*), trailing mallow, and many members of the mint family, including spearmint, coyote mint, and lemon balm. All but the western nettle produce showy flowers. Western and stinging nettle are wind-pollinated and produce nondescript blooms. Western nettle is found in moister soils than stinging nettle, and it is wispier and smaller with leaves that are more scalloped than serrated. Western nettle also has tiny raised dots on its leaves

NOTES: Although a widespread skin irritant, stinging nettle is included as an edible (page 90) because of its many fantastic qualities. With that said, anyone hiking within 80 miles of the coast should be aware of this plant. Brushing up against nettle with bare skin will lead to its tiny stinging hairs pricking your skin. Every prick can cause severe itching and discomfort. The pricked skin will have tiny, red swollen dots. The pain and redness lasts 15–30 minutes. Interestingly, stinging nettle was once used for arthritis relief; those afflicted would brush branches across impacted areas, endure the discomfort for 20 minutes, and feel much better afterwards. This may have worked because nettle increases blood flow and induces a pain-reducing response.

WATER HEMLOCK
(Cicuta spp.*)*

WILD

TYPE: Perennial
STATUS: Native
LEAF ARRANGEMENT: Opposite, odd-pinnate, and lance-like
POISONOUS PARTS: All parts are toxic to eat.

HABITAT: Water hemlock is hardly widespread, which makes it even more dangerous—no one ever expects it. It grows along ponds and slowing-moving streams. Although it can be found high in the San Bernardino Mountains, it prefers the coasts of Santa Barbara, Los Angeles, and San Diego Counties.

GROWTH: This is a lush-looking plant that grows between 2.5 and 4 feet tall and half as wide. It is an upright grower with fleshy, hollow stems. The axis where the leaf joins the branch is tinged purple or red. Its stalks have much variation; they might be light green, purple, or red, and the coloration might be uniform, spotted, or stripped.

LEAVES: Water hemlock's leaves are comprised of many leaflets (odd-pinnate). The entire ensemble is triangular in shape. Each leaflet is lance- or oval-shaped, 1–4 inches long, and has serrated edges. Leaves are generally a shiny forest green.

FLOWERS: Gracefully rising above the foliage in creamy clusters of white, water hemlock's flowers are beautiful, like all flowers in the carrot/parsley family. They are technically a compound umbel, an array of umbrella-shaped clusters of tiny flowers. The individual umbels of the tiny flowers look almost ball-like.

OTHER NAMES: Spotted cowbane

chervil   wild carrot   wild celery

COMPARABLE SPECIES: Its umbel flowers, upright growth, and pinnate leaves resemble chervil (*Anthriscus* spp.), wild carrot (*Daucus* spp.), and wild celery (*Apium graveolens*, page 214). Chervil leaflets are finely divided, not lance-like. Wild carrot leaves and stems are slightly bristly, not smooth, and its leaves are finer, not lance-like. Wild celery has the familiar celery stalk, not round or smooth, and its leaves and stalks have a pleasant celery-like smell.

NOTES: All parts of this plant are poisonous. If ingested, water hemlock will cause nausea, vomiting, convulsions, and even death.

DEATH CAMAS
(Toxicoscordion spp.)

WILD

TYPE: Bulbous perennial and deciduous herb
STATUS: Native
LEAF ARRANGEMENT: Basal and bulb-like
POISONOUS PARTS: All parts

HABITAT: Five members of this genus can be found in Southern California. From right along the coast and the Channel Islands up to elevations of 9,000 feet and throughout the hilly parts of the deserts, death camas is widespread, but only found in the wild. They tolerate shallow and acidic soils well.

GROWTH: Leaves and flower spikes grow from bulbs that are about 1 inch wide. Death camas is not a voracious grower and will get lanky and spindly at times. Leaves tend to flop over as soils dry. Its tall creamy flower spikes are its most distinguishing attribute.

LEAVES: Narrow, flat, and typically folded in the middle, death camas leaves are 4–18 inches long and 0.25–1 inch wide. They are a deep forest green to pale green. Older plants will die back to the bulb every year.

GREENS

Foraging for greens starts where it did eons ago—with plants that adapted to follow humans. Our presence creates conditions that favor certain plants, and they favor us in turn. Most of the plants in this section are non-native people-followers—and all provide phenomenal nutrition and great eating.

Foraged greens look and taste different than store-bought greens. They are not as sexy, that's for sure. These greens may have damage from herbivores, and they may be discolored or disheveled. And as the season wanes, foraged greens become coarse and bitter. None of these facts, however, should dissuade you from foraging for them, because foraged greens are far more nutritious and fresher than any green from a store.

TIPS FOR FORAGING HEALTHY GREENS:

- Avoid greens found along roads. The toxic exhaust and fine particulate pollution produced by cars and trucks accumulates in greens. Never harvest within 50 feet of a road. Moreover, always try to forage on the windward side of urban features.

- Avoid greens in/near industrial areas or where you suspect toxins.

- Always perform a quick taste test before harvesting. Sometimes the younger leaves are tastier, as in the case of mustard and radish. But sometimes the opposite is true, as in the case of New Zealand spinach and wild celery.

- Greens generally taste better in the spring. As the season wanes, it's often necessary to lightly sear, boil, or steam the greens.

- Don't pull up the entire plant. Either cut off leaves or pull them off as needed. Most of these plants, especially invasive weeds, can be cut to within 6 inches of the ground. Pulling the entire plant speeds topsoil loss.

- And lastly, see page 10 so you can recognize signs of pesticide use—never harvest if the use of pesticides is suspected!

BURNET, SALAD
(Sanguisorba minor)

WILD

TYPE: Spreading perennial
STATUS: Non-native
LEAF ARRANGEMENT: Grows in a rosette; leaves are oval, arranged oppositely, and sometimes oblong with serrated edges
HARVEST TIME: Winter and spring

HABITAT: This spreading perennial is a people-follower and prefers light shade (never full shade) and at least a little moisture. From Palo Verde to San Bernardino, it is more likely to be found in the foothills and low mountains than immediately along the coast or in the desert. It tolerates salty soils and is not uncommon in areas irrigated with reclaimed water. It can also be found in nurseries and edible gardens.

GROWTH: Salad burnet grows as a rosette (stalks growing out from its fleshy center) and can reach 8 inches tall if not trampled upon. If found under equipment or on a surface where people walk, it will grow as a prostrate ground cover. Its stems root with soil contact, and it might sprawl for over 2 feet.

LEAVES: One leaf stalk is comprised of 4–12 pairs of separate leaves growing oppositely. Leaves are oval, sometimes oblong, and distinctly serrated. They are 1 inch long, grow from tiny stems (petioles), and are a rich forest green.

FLOWERS: The flower head is an oblong ball that sways on a reddish stem. Flower stalks can reach to 18 inches tall. Each ball is comprised of many small flowers that start out as green and change to a pastel crimson, magenta, or pink. It blooms in summer.

SEASON: Late winter to early spring is the best time for young, tasty leaves. However, salad burnet can be eaten anytime it is found; the leaves just might be more bitter later in the year.

BENEFITS: Salad burnet has been used for centuries as both a food and medicine. Experts claim it has anti-inflammatory and antioxidant properties.

OTHER NAMES: Garden burnet, small burnet

stinging nettle

COMPARABLE SPECIES: Stinging nettle (page 90) has serrated leaves that look a lot like those of salad burnet. However, stinging nettle's leaves are lance-like, come to a pronounced point, and grow upright on semi-woody stems. Salad burnet is a flopping plant without pointy leaves.

NOTES: Young leaves are tasty, and the flavor ranges from a sweet cucumber to tart. Older leaves are bitter. Leaves are eaten raw, added to drinks, or combined with stews and soups.

CHICKWEED
(Stellaria media)

WILD

TYPE: Small fleshy annual
STATUS: Non-native
LEAF ARRANGEMENT: Opposite
HARVEST TIME: From the first rains until the soil dries out in early summer; chickweed can be found year-round in irrigated areas.

HABITAT: Chickweed is a people-follower and is common in shaded urban areas, such as around buildings, in planter boxes, or around campsites under a grove of trees. Not a desert weed, it prefers the coastal influence and is rarely found on the eastern side of the mountains. Chickweed likes crevices and corners.

GROWTH: Small and petite, this annual tumbles along the ground, growing 3–18 inches tall.

LEAVES: The leaves are opposite and oblong with a pronounced point at the end. Leaves average between 0.5 and 1 inch in size and are somewhat shiny and a rich-to-muted green.

FLOWERS: Resembling a little white star with 4 or 5 thin narrow petals that are no longer than 0.25 inch, this beautiful flower is easy to miss. The stems (petioles) are thin, delicate, and as green as the leaves.

SEASON: This plant can be harvested anytime. It will die back by summer in areas without irrigation or coastal moisture. If there's moisture, it's a year-round crop.

BENEFITS: Chickweed is a superfood. It is high in beta-carotene, calcium, chlorophyll, iron, magnesium, potassium, riboflavin, vitamin C, and zinc. Chickweed is an anti-inflammatory and an antioxidant, and it promotes a healthy lymphatic system. It is also used externally to help heal skin problems, including poison oak dermatitis.

OTHER NAMES: None

petty spurge   Scarlet pimpernel

COMPARABLE SPECIES: The plants that most resemble chickweed are petty spurge (*Euphorbia peplus*, page 32) and Scarlet pimpernel (*Lysimachia arvensis*). Petty spurge's delicate leaf structure and its low-growing nature lead it to be mistaken for chickweed often. All Euphorbias are poisonous, and all have milky sap—always break open a stem and examine the sap before harvesting chickweed. Another difference is the flower: chickweed has a white star; spurge's is either green or yellow and circle-like. Scarlet pimpernel is identified by its orange flower, tall growth, and highly ridged (almost square) stem.

NOTES: Leaves and seeds can be eaten raw or cooked. The taste is bland and goes well with stronger flavors, such as mustard and wild radish. Just grab the plant and cut it down to 4 inches off the ground. Leaves and flowers are the best parts to harvest; the stems can be chewy.

Dayflower

DAYFLOWER AND
SMALL LEAF SPIDERWORT
(*Commelina benghalensis* and *Tradescantia fluminensis*)

WILD ORNAMENTAL

TYPE: Spreading perennial
STATUS: Non-native
LEAF ARRANGEMENT: Alternate; leaves are oval and trailing
HARVEST TIME: Early spring is best, but it can be harvested all year.

HABITAT: These spreading, rooting fleshy perennials are common in urban-influenced areas. They prefer above-freezing temperatures, moisture, and filtered shade. Dayflower is often planted for erosion control and easy to find within 70 miles of the coast.

GROWTH: These two plants belong to the spiderwort family. They might get to 2 feet tall and be found as a small patch of stems and leaves, or as a sprawling mass covering hundreds of square feet. When trampled or disturbed, they are no more than 4 inches tall. Their fleshy stems root at the joints when they make soil contact. The stems are notable for their knobby joints.

LEAVES: Leaves are oval or oblong and 1–2.5 inches long; they clasp onto the fleshy stems (they lack a petiole). The leaves are attached alternately, and their veins run parallel with the midrib. The margins of the dayflower are wavy; spiderwort has smooth edges. Leaf color ranges from pale green to grass green.

FLOWERS: All members of the spiderwort family have flowers with 3 petals. The dayflower's blooms are a rich sky-blue and about 0.5 inch across, with the two upper petals larger than the lower one, which might be a pale blue or white. It blooms May through September. The small-leaf spiderwort has white flowers, about 0.5 inch wide, and all the petals are the same size, creating a star-like appearance. It blooms April through July and intermittently afterwards.

SEASON: Collect it from winter through spring, but it produces new growth nearly all year.

BENEFITS: These plants are known as famine foods in many parts of the world and are consumed when food runs short. They have good amounts of protein and vitamins B and C. They have some antioxidant and anti-inflammatory qualities.

OTHER NAMES: *Commelina benghalensis* is also known as tropical spiderwort. *Tradescantia fluminensis* is known as wandering Jew or inch plant.

ivy   periwinkle

COMPARABLE SPECIES: The only other low-growing ground covers that resemble these spiderworts are ivy (*Hedera* spp., page 18) and periwinkle (*Vinca* spp.) both of which can are found growing in the same environments. Spiderworts are distinguished by their knobby, brittle stems and the parallel veins in their leaves.

NOTES: Young leaves and shoots are eaten raw or cooked. The flowers are edible too. The taste is bland to fibrous.

DOCK, CURLY
(Rumex crispus)

WILD

TYPE: Perennial
STATUS: Non-native
LEAF ARRANGEMENT: Basal growth
HARVEST TIME: Midwinter to mid-spring

HABITAT: Curly dock prefers slightly acidic soil, moderate rainfall, and the protection from the extremes found in deserts and mountaintops. It can be found in public parks, near campsites, and on college campuses.

GROWTH: This clumping perennial mostly consists of leaves, and under the right conditions it can create a formidable mass, spreading to 2 feet across. Generally, it is much smaller.

LEAVES: Curly dock is distinguished by its dull green, long, elliptical or oblong leaf and its wavy margins. In winter and spring the leaves get to 18 inches long; by midsummer they flop over and are 10 inches long. The central vein in the leaf is typically a pale greenish white and sometimes reddish at its base.

FLOWERS: Curly dock's mass of small flowers radiates from stalks that are 2–4 feet tall. The blossoms are wind-pollinated and not showy. Flowers start out a light green, turn to pale yellow, ripen to a rusty, pinkish red, and mature to mahogany brown. The flower stalks have leaves on their lower half.

SEASON: Midwinter to mid-spring are the best times to harvest the tender new leaves.

BENEFITS: Curly dock is high in vitamins A and C, iron, and potassium. It also has protein. Curly dock has been used for centuries as a medicinal plant. Most of the other species in curly dock's genus (*Rumex*, the docks and sorrels) are edible, and not just the leaves, but roots and seeds too.

OTHER NAMES: Rhubarb (though cultivated rhubarb is in a different genus).

plantain   yerba mansa   wild rhubarb

COMPARABLE SPECIES: Luckily, the plants that resemble curly dock are edible. Plantain (*Plantago major*, page 76) has large veins that run parallel with the leaf stem. Yerba mansa (*Anemopsis californica*) has a much thicker leaf than plantain and a bitter fragrance when crushed or torn. And wild rhubarb (*Rumex hymenosepalus*, page 82) has a distinct yellow or red stem and the leaf is bluish with wavy edges, but it is only edible after boiling.

NOTES: Curly dock's leaves can be eaten raw, boiled, roasted, or steamed. They are bitter, chewy, and delicious, especially in salads with toppings such as cheese or nuts. If eating in the summer or the fall, plan on lightly searing the leaves to remove some of the bitterness and acids.

LONDON ROCKET
(Sisymbrium irio)

WILD

TYPE: Annual
STATUS: Non-native
LEAF ARRANGEMENT: Leaves are pinnately lobed and alternate
HARVEST TIME: Late fall to early spring

HABITAT: This mustard relative and spindly annual is one of the most abundant weeds in Southern California and can be found from the coast to the mountains to the desert. It tolerates a wide range of soil and moisture conditions, although it is found more often in full sun than in full shade. It does not do well in compacted soils.

GROWTH: London rocket ranges from 9 inches to 2.5 feet tall on erect, but slender, stems, making the plant prone to swaying. It is a bit rangy and grows 1–2 feet wide. When young it grows basally, but it sends up leaves and flower stalks as it ages.

LEAVES: The leaves are pinnately lobed (one leaf looks like a bunch of smaller ones growing from one stem), and the lobed portions resemble narrow arrowheads, some of which have flares or wings at the blunt end. The lobes are toothed. There are 1–7 pairs of lobes per stem and they are alternate. Each leaf is 1–6 inches long and a rich deep green.

FLOWERS: Tiny yellow flowers grow en masse on long stems originating from the main stalk. The stems can reach 2.5 feet tall. Each flower has four petals and blooms January to April.

SEEDPODS: They are needle-like and 1–2 inches long. They generally point upward or outward. Seedpods are a muted green.

SEASON: Harvest London rocket from late fall through early spring. This is one of the first annuals to sprout following a rain, and it is a reliable green in winter.

BENEFITS: Like mustard, London rocket is rich in nutrients, vitamins, and fiber. It is an antioxidant and an anti-inflammatory. Its tender stems, flowers, and seeds are also edible.

OTHER NAMES: Tumble mustard

wintercress   yellow rocket   mustard   wallflower

COMPARABLE SPECIES: Many species have flowers that look similar to London rocket, including wintercress and yellow rocket (*Barbarea* spp.), mustard (*Brassica* spp., page 54), and wallflower (*Erysimum* spp.). Examining the leaves is the easiest way to distinguish between London rocket and the look-alikes; none of the plants mentioned above have pinnately lobed leaves.

NOTES: Leaves are edible raw or cooked. It is healthiest to pick the lower leaves. Naturally, young plants are more palatable than old.

PEPPERWEED
(Lepidium spp.)

WILD

TYPE: Annual and perennial
STATUS: Native and non-native
LEAF ARRANGEMENT: Basal and alternate along the stem
HARVEST TIME: January through July

HABITAT: Found from sea level to elevations of 9,000 feet and into the low desert, pepperweed is well adapted. This common group of species tolerates a range of soil acidity, salinity, and moisture levels—*L. fremontii* can be found in areas that get as little as 5 inches of rain per year. All varieties seem to prefer coarse and/or deep soils. Native species are easier to find than non-natives.

GROWTH: This is one of the first plants to produce foliage and flowers after the first rain or the spring thaw. Pepperweed belongs to the mustard family. Although there is a great deal of variation between these species, all pepperweed species have tiny hairs along the stems and leaves; many 4-petaled tiny, white saucer-like flowers; and winged fruit, which is small, flat, round, and notched. They grow between 6 inches and 2 feet tall (*L. latifolium* gets to 4 feet), are multi-branched, and a bit rangy looking.

LEAVES: The oval, oblong, lance-like or spoon-shaped leaves are 1–6 inches long. They are more linear along the stem, but more pinnately or slightly lobed at the base. They are hairy with small serrations on the margins. Color ranges from pale green to rich green and bluish green.

FLOWERS: The flowers are white and saucer-shaped, with 4 petals that are no more than 0.06 inch across. They occur in the familiar mustard-like cluster—a profusion of tiny flowers at the top of a stalk or stem (raceme) and with a small, round flat fruit (some of which are notched) below them. They bloom as early as January along the coast, in February in the desert, and in March in the mountains.

SEASON: January through June.

BENEFITS: Besides chlorophyll and fiber, the leaves of pepperweed also provide iron and vitamins A and C.

OTHER NAMES: Peppergrass

shepherd's purse

COMPARABLE SPECIES: Given its rangy nature, pepperweed is mostly confused with the other edible mustards. Its flowers most resemble shepherd's purse (page 200).

NOTES: The entire plant is edible: leaves, flowers, seeds, and roots. It can be eaten raw or cooked, but it has a pungent and strong peppery flavor. The most common varieties are *L. fremontii*, a native perennial found throughout the desert in elevations above 1,500 feet, *L. lasiocarpum*, a native annual found throughout the desert, from the lowlands to elevations of 4,000 feet, and *L. latifolium*, a non-native perennial found in nearly all of the wetlands along the coast. *L. virginicum* is a native annual found along the coast and up to 100 miles inland.

PLANTAIN, COMMON
(Plantago major)

WILD

TYPE: Fleshy perennial
STATUS: Non-native
LEAF ARRANGEMENT: Rosette of basal leaves
HARVEST TIME: Anytime you spot it

HABITAT: A people-follower and easy to find, it is abundant in Southern California. Plantain prefers clay and moist soils. It can be found in urban lots, shaded areas, along moist hiking trails, and on college campuses.

GROWTH: Leaves emerge from a central clump (basal growth). As the leaves age, they flop over; it rarely gets taller than 1 foot.

LEAVES: The dark green leaves can range from 4 inches to 1 foot long and 1–5 inches wide. The shape can be described as oblong, elliptical, or even oval. The tips are either pointed or rounded. Its distinguishing attribute is the large veins that run parallel to the leaf stem. Young leaves are narrow, lance-like, and heavily dimpled.

FLOWERS: A sturdy flower stalk shoots up from the middle of the flopping leaves. The stiff stalks can reach up to 18 inches, but most are shorter. Flowers bloom April–September.

SEASON: The best times to harvest are spring through early summer, but the plant doesn't go dormant until the first frost, which means it is a year-round edible in frost-free, moist areas.

BENEFITS: Plantain is a superfood. The leaves are very high in calcium, fiber, and vitamin A (beta carotene). They are also high in vitamins C and K. They have mild anti-inflammatory and antimicrobial properties and are excellent for healing wounds; plantain salves are reputed to reduce the severity of inflammation, rashes, and sunburns.

OTHER NAMES: Broadleaf plantain, white man's footprint

curly dock   wild rhubarb   yerba mansa

COMPARABLE SPECIES: Plantain has parallel veins, which make it distinct when compared to similar plants. Luckily, the plants that resemble plantain are non-toxic. Curly dock (*Rumex crispus*, page 70) is distinguished by its dull green lance-like leaf and wavy, slightly lobed edges. It is delicious. Wild rhubarb (*Rumex hymenosepalus*, page 82) has a distinct yellow or red stem, and the leaf is bluish with wavy edges. It is edible. And yerba mansa (*Anemopsis californica*) has a much thicker leaf than plantain and a bitter fragrance when crushed or torn. This plant is more often used as medicine than food.

NOTES: Young leaves can be eaten raw, and older ones are cooked. Older leaves are often chewy and taste strongly like spinach. Tea from the leaves is purported to promote healthy skin.

PRICKLY LETTUCE
(Lactuca serriola)

WILD

TYPE: Annual

STATUS: Non-native

LEAF ARRANGEMENT: Leaves are alternate and linear or deeply lobed

HARVEST TIME: Late fall through early spring

HABITAT: This successful weed is a people-follower and can be found anywhere that gets at least 10 inches of rainfall per year. It tolerates salty soil, poor soil, and compaction. Prickly lettuce is widespread and can be found near agricultural areas, utility easements, residential properties, and public parks.

GROWTH: Thriving in cool seasons, this annual is one of the first weeds to sprout after the first fall rain or the last frost of spring. Height varies greatly and ranges from 1.5 to 8 feet tall. It can be 6–14 inches wide. Young leaves grow from a basal clump; as it matures, it grows skyward on rigid stems.

LEAVES: To identify this annual, look for its prickly edges, the bristles on the underside along the midrib, its alternate arrangement, and its milky sap (latex). The leaves clasp directly to stalks (there are no petioles). Interestingly, the leaves twist to maximize or reduce sun exposure. Older leaves of prickly lettuce are pinnately lobed; younger leaves are linear, long, and have blunt ends.

FLOWERS: Flower stalks are upright and hold a cluster of ray-like pale yellow flowers 0.5–0.75 inch wide. Flowers mature to seed puffs that resemble a dandelion. It blooms May through September.

SEASON: Along the coast the season starts with the first fall rains in November. In the mountains the season starts after the last frost, in February or March.

BENEFITS: The leaves have some fiber and nutrients.

OTHER NAMES: Wild lettuce, compass plant

sow thistle

COMPARABLE SPECIES: Young prickly lettuce looks somewhat similar to sow thistle (*Sonchus* spp., page 88), which is edible and related. However, sow thistle lacks the small spines on the underside of the leaf along the midrib.

NOTES: Only the young leaves are palatable. As the plant matures, the leaves become tough, prickly, and bitter. Young leaves are eaten raw or lightly cooked.

PURSLANE, COMMON
(Portulaca oleracea)

WILD

TYPE: Fleshy annual
STATUS: Non-native
LEAF ARRANGEMENT: Slightly alternate
HARVEST TIME: When the plant is actively growing, usually in the months following winter rains

HABITAT: Purslane is a people-follower, and the greater an area's population, the better your chances of finding it. Although more common west of the mountains, purslane can be found in the desert too. It prefers filtered areas or full sun, incidental irrigation, and human disturbance, like hoeing. Purslane can be found along the margins of agriculture, in picnic areas, and in urban landscapes.

GROWTH: With pinkish red trailing stems, small succulent leaves, and a low-growing manner, it is fairly easy to identify. It rarely gets larger than 6 inches high or 1.5 feet wide.

LEAVES: The small leaves are obovate (shaped like a tiny tennis racket) and between 0.25 and 0.75 inch long. On casual observation the leaves look like they grow oppositely, but on closer inspection they are slightly alternate. Its stems grow to 10 inches long.

SEASON: New growth found after the winter rains tastes the sweetest, but the plant's leaves and stems can be eaten throughout its life. In frost-free areas with moderate moisture, you can find this plant year-round.

BENEFITS: Purslane is high in nearly all the essential nutrients, including iron, omega-3s, and vitamin E. Nutritionally, it can easily supplant any big leafy green.

OTHER NAMES: Duckweed, little hogweed, and wild portulaca

graceful sandmat   spotted spurge

COMPARABLE SPECIES: The plants that most resemble purslane belong to the genus Euphorbia, and all are poisonous. Graceful sandmat (*Euphorbia hypericifolia*, page 32) and spotted spurge (*E. maculata*, page 32) have red stems, tiny leaves, and are also low-growing. Both these weeds can be found growing alongside purslane. Luckily, identification is easy: break a stem. *Euphorbia* species have milky sap; purslane has watery, clear sap. These spurges have super-tiny white flowers, while purslane has tiny pale yellow flowers.

NOTES: Purslane is a staple of foraged greens. Eat the young leaves and the stem, but make sure to wash it thoroughly. It has a tart, lemony kick and is perfect with the stronger greens, such as mustard and nasturtium. Purslane can be added to eggs or juices, or lightly cooked by itself. Many grocery stores in California also sell purslane.

RHUBARB, WILD
(Rumex hymenosepalus)

WILD

TYPE: Perennial herb
STATUS: Native
LEAF ARRANGEMENT: Alternate, but looks like a basal grower
HARVEST TIME: Winter and spring

HABITAT: This is one of the few greens you can find in the desert, although not at the lowest elevations. Wild rhubarb prefers slightly alkaline soils that are rocky and have very little salt. It is more likely to be found in the foothills than on the plains.

GROWTH: This native plant often resembles a fleshy, tough mass of leaves. It will reach 1–3 feet tall and just as wide. The stems at the base become reddish with age.

LEAVES: The lance-like or oblong leaves are 3–12 inches long and 0.75–3 inches wide. The edges are generally wavy. While this perennial looks a lot like Curly dock (*Rumex crispus*, page 70), wild rhubarb's leaves are different: they're a more-pale bluish green, opposed to deep green; the leaves are also not as long, nor are they richly veined like curly dock's.

FLOWERS: Wild rhubarb's flowers consist of tiny balls attached to small stems on the plant's stout stalks; these rise above the foliage, creating a plume-like display. These stalks can reach 3 feet tall, with the flower head up to 1 foot long, but most are smaller. The blossoms are wind-pollinated and not showy. Flowers start out light green, turn a pinkish red, and mature to a rust-red brown. It blooms January to May.

SEASON: Early winter is best, but it can be cooked anytime it's found.

BENEFITS: Like the other *Rumex* species (page 86 and 70), it is high in iron, potassium, and vitamins A and C. It also includes some protein, and its seeds are edible too.

OTHER NAMES: Canaigre dock

| plantain | curly dock | yerba mansa | sea lavender |

COMPARABLE SPECIES: Plantain (*Plantago major*, page 83) is edible and has large veins that run parallel to the leaf stem. Curly dock (*Rumex crispus*, page 70) is edible and has longer and greener leaves. Yerba mansa (*Anemopsis californica*) is medicinal and has a much thicker leaf and a bitter fragrance when crushed or torn. And Sea Lavender (*Limonium sventenii and L. perezii*) has the same bluish leaf, but lacks the reddish lower stalk and has beautiful blue blooms.

NOTES: Wild rhubarb has been eaten for centuries, mostly because it can be found in areas with few other greens. Although it can be eaten raw, it's far better cooked—the leaves are bitter. Boil the leaves in several changes of water, which helps remove the plant's tannins.

SALTBUSH, BIG

(Atriplex lentiformis)

WILD

TYPE: Shrub

STATUS: Native

LEAF ARRANGEMENT: Leaves are typically oppositely attached; leaves are attached on petioles that are 0.5 inch long or less

HARVEST TIME: Late fall through early spring

HABITAT: Fairly widespread in Southern California, big saltbush grows in dry, poor, and saline soils. Prevalent along the coast, it can also be found in a majority of the inland foothills, ravines, and washes, along with the eastern sides of desert hills. It rarely grows higher than elevations of 2,000 feet.

GROWTH: This rangy looking shrub branches both upward and outward, becoming 2.5–10 feet tall and just as wide. It is semi-deciduous in the summer, when its outer growth dies back, leaving a mass of prickly, spine-like twigs.

LEAVES: Saltbush's leaves are oblong and spear-shaped with wavy margins; they are noticeably veined. The leaves are a pale bluish green to gray-green and 0.5–2.5 inches long on small, but stout, stems.

FLOWERS: Plume-like and growing from the ends of branches, saltbush's flowers are wind-pollinated; a mass of tiny balls start out green, ripen to pale pink-maroon, and mature to a straw yellow. It blooms in June through August.

SEASON: This plant grows best in the cooler season; succulent young growth is found December through April.

BENEFITS: Saltbush is not a foraging staple, but it's a good species to know about because it's often the only edible plant found in its habitat. It does contain minerals, nutrients, and vitamins, but not in great amounts. Seeds contain good amounts of protein.

OTHER NAMES: Orache, quail bush

brittlebush   nightshade   lambsquarters   goosefoot   pigweed

COMPARABLE SPECIES: The plants that resemble saltbush have spear-like or triangular leaves. Brittlebush (*Encelia* spp.) is similar, but its leaves have resins that smell awful. Nightshade (page 114) is comparable, but the leaf is greener and the plant spindly. And saltbush resembles lambsquarters (page 52), goosefoot (page 52), and pigweed (page 178) when young, and all three are edible.

NOTES: Saltbush belongs to the amaranth/goosefoot family. The salty leaves and fleshy young shoots can be eaten raw, but they are better lightly cooked or added to other dishes. Dry seeds are pounded and used as a grain-like meal.

SORREL, SHEEP
(Rumex acetosella)

WILD

TYPE: Perennial herb
STATUS: Non-native
LEAF ARRANGEMENT: Basal growth
HARVEST TIME: Late winter through early summer, although it can be eaten anytime it is found

HABITAT: Sheep sorrel is not widely distributed in Southern California, but it can be found in the mountains at higher altitudes—up to 9,000 feet. It prefers moderate moisture and acidic, deep soils with little salinity (and that's why it is not widespread). It's not likely to be found in dense shade.

GROWTH: This fleshy perennial can reach 2 feet tall and 8 inches wide, although most specimens are smaller. It colonizes an area via underground stems (rhizomes) and seeds. Leaves are rarely longer than 2 inches. Stems and stalks are green when young and reddish with age.

LEAVES: Sheep sorrel's leaf looks like a dagger and has a narrow oblong shape with a pronounced point at the tip, and a flair at the stem-end that looks like a handguard (this is known as a hastate). It is 0.75–2.25

inches long and 0.5 inch wide. Leaves grow from the base, from the underground roots, and along the flower stalk. Its leaves are grass green to deep green, and only the midvein is pronounced.

FLOWERS: Flower stalks proudly stand above the plant. Each stalk is comprised of many stems, and each stem has many tiny, ball-like flowers. They are wind-pollinated and start out a light green, maturing to a rusty red. It blooms from March to the first freeze.

SEASON: Late winter through early summer are best, although it can be eaten anytime it is found.

BENEFITS: The leaf is not a powerhouse of nutrition, but it will provide fiber, fatty acids, and vitamin K when nothing else can be found.

OTHER NAMES: Sorrel, garden sorrel, sour dock

Mexican evening primrose

COMPARABLE SPECIES: When young, it may look like Mexican evening primrose (*Oenothera speciosa*, page 162), which is widespread in urbanized areas. The difference is in the leaf margins: sheep sorrel has smooth margins, the primrose's are toothed. Mexican evening primrose is considered edible.

NOTES: In Latin, the word *acetum* means "vinegar," and sheep sorrel gets its species name from the bitter, sour taste of its leaves. They are eaten raw or cooked and are a great addition to other concoctions. The younger the leaf, the better the flavor.

SOW THISTLE
(*Sonchus* spp.)

TYPE: Annual
STATUS: Non-native
LEAF ARRANGEMENT: Leaves are alternately attached but basal at the plant's base; the leaves are oblong or lance-like
HARVEST TIME: Late winter, early spring

WILD

HABITAT: There are at least 5 species of *Sonchus* growing in Southern California, and all are people-followers. From the coast and the mountains to the desert, sow thistle can be found everywhere—in urban areas, public parks, and state parks. It prefers shallow soils, tolerates salts, and can be found in dry soils with shade, or in moist soils with full sun.

GROWTH: Sow thistle can range from a low-growing plant that is about 4 inches tall to plants reaching 3 feet tall. These quick-growing annuals rarely get more than 1 foot wide, however. Its most distinguishing characteristics are its hollow stems and milky sap.

LEAVES: The leaves are a lackluster green, prickly, and have many soft and thin segments, making them distinct; the leaves are 3–8 inches long.

The leaf margins tend to be lightly toothed. The stems and stalks tend to be a darker green than the leaf and some have reddish overtones.

FLOWERS: The flowers look like a dandelion: bright yellow and composite. They range in width from 0.25 to 0.5 inch. All varieties bloom in early winter, but some bloom year-round.

SEASON: Spring is the best time for moist, easy-to-digest leaves, but sow thistle can be harvested anytime it is found, which is nearly year-round in many areas.

BENEFITS: Because of its abundance, sow thistle is a staple of foraging in Southern California. It is not a superfood, but it does have beneficial amounts of minerals, vitamin C, and fiber. The root, like dandelion, can be roasted and used to make tea.

OTHER NAMES: Field sow thistle, moist sow thistle, prickly sow thistle, spiny sow thistle

dandelion

COMPARABLE SPECIES: When young, sow thistle may look like the related cat's ear and dandelion (page 46), but dandelion leaves grow from the base, and the plant stays low to the ground. Sow thistle leaves grow both from the base and along the stalk, and it is far taller.

NOTES: Leaves are eaten raw or lightly seared. Stems, petals, and roots are edible too. The leaves taste like lettuce.

STINGING NETTLE
(Urtica spp.)

WILD

TYPE: Annual and perennial
STATUS: Native and non-native
LEAF ARRANGEMENT: Opposite; leaf margins are oblong and fiercely serrated
HARVEST TIME: Anytime

WARNING: If you brush against it with bare skin, the leaves will sting you, causing intense discomfort.

HABITAT: Any area that gets at least 11 inches of rain per year and is within 100 miles of the coast could be home to stinging nettle. It thrives near human development. It is also found along the ocean, at elevations of up to 8,000 feet, as well as on the eastern side of the more coastal mountains. It peters out in the low desert. It is more likely found under trees than in full sun.

GROWTH: An erect branching annual or perennial, nettles become some-what woody. They range in height from 4 inches to 2 feet and have single- or multi-branched stems.

LEAVES: Nettle leaves are distinctly oblong or spear-like; the edges are uniquely serrated, resembling piranha teeth. Each leaf is 0.75–2 inches long, attached with small stems, and found opposite another leaf. The color of the leaves ranges from pale green to forest green.

FLOWERS: Tiny wind-pollinated flowers form on small wispy stems from the axis of the leaves and stalks. They range in color from green to brown. Varieties in coastal areas bloom January–April; in the mountains, they bloom May–September.

SEASON: Late winter through spring, or anytime before the plant flowers

BENEFITS: Stinging nettle leaves are a superfood. They are rich in chlorophyll, calcium, iron, magnesium, and potassium, as well as vitamins A, C, D, and K. Stinging nettle leaves are reputed to have anti-inflammatory properties, reduce the severity of allergies, and improve bone and joint health.

OTHER NAMES: Nettle

western nettle   hairy beggarticks   trailing mallow   coyote mint   lemon balm

COMPARABLE SPECIES: The leaves of stinging nettle resemble many edible plants, including western nettle (*Hesperocnide tenella*), hairy beggarticks (*Bidens pilosa*), trailing mallow, and members of the mint family, including spearmint, coyote mint, and lemon balm. All but western nettle produce showy flowers. Western and stinging nettle are wind-pollinated and produce nondescript blooms. Western nettle is found in moister soils than stinging nettle and is wispier and smaller with leaves that are more scalloped than serrated. Western nettle also has tiny raised dots on its leaves.

NOTES: You will need gloves to harvest the leaves. Even brushing up against the plant can cause mild to severe itching for 15–30 minutes. Drying, soaking leaves in water, or cooking eliminates the stinging chemicals. Leaves are either added to dishes or used to make tea. The leaves taste like spinach. Young leaves have fewer nitrates and are healthier.

THISTLE, RUSSIAN
(Salsola australis and *Salsola tragus)*

WILD

TYPE: Annual
STATUS: Non-native
LEAF ARRANGEMENT: Opposite and alternate leaves that resemble thorns
HARVEST TIME: Late winter through spring

WARNING: The small barbs cause stinging and discomfort if eaten raw or handled.

HABITAT: This aggressive annual dominates Southern California; it is often seen as a harbinger of a warming and less-hospitable environment. Commonly known as the tumbleweed, it grows where other weeds can't.

GROWTH: Russian thistle's wiry reddish branches grow from a small trunk. It is 2–5 feet tall and just as wide. In late winter and spring it is a blue, dense green mass, but by summer it starts losing its leaves and becomes airy looking. Unless irrigated, it completes its life cycle by October, when the strong Santa Ana winds blow it off its perch, and it begins to tumble.

LEAVES: This plant's leaves evolved to reduce predation, and they are barb-like with spines at their tips. The upper leaves are succulent, thin, and cylindrical, sometimes growing to 2 inches long. They are also deciduous. The lower leaves are thicker, 1 inch long, and persist until the plant dies.

FLOWERS: Tiny white, pink, or maroon flowers sit in the axis of stems and provide a hint of beauty when they flower. They are wind-pollinated. *Salsola tragus* blooms July to October, and *S. australis* flowers nearly all year long.

SEASON: Late winter through spring

BENEFITS: Russian thistle is a member of the amaranth family, and like them, it is rich in minerals, phosphorus, and vitamin A. It also has good amounts of amino acids and protein.

OTHER NAMES: Prickly saltwort, tumbleweed, windwitch

COMPARABLE SPECIES: There are no comparable species.

NOTES: Cut off the tips of stems or 4–6 inches of the young shoots; these can be eaten raw or boiled, sautéed, or added to other dishes. The best stems are supple and generally bluish green, not yellowish green. The seeds are also edible.

Other Plants with Edible Greens

Blackberry *Rubus* spp. (page 98)

Black medick *Medicago lupulina* (page 176)

Bulrush *Bolboschoenus* spp. and *Schoenoplectus* spp. (page 212)

Cattail *Typha* spp. (page 42)

Cheeseweed *Malva parviflora* (page 44)

Chicory *Cichorium intybus* (page 196)

Clover *Trifolium* spp. (page 152)

Dandelion *Taraxacum* spp. (page 46)

Fennel, sweet *Foeniculum vulgare* (page 48)

Filaree, red-stemmed *Erodium cicutarium* (page 50)

Grape, wild *Vitis californica* and *V. girdiana* (page 104)

Henbit *Lamium amplexicaule* (page 154)

Lambsquarters and goosefoot *Chenopodium album* and *C. murale* (page 52)

Macroalgae: kelp and seaweed (page 230)

Miner's lettuce *Claytonia perfoliata* (page 216)

Mustard *Brassica* spp. (page 54)

New Zealand spinach *Tetragonia tetragonioides* (page 226)

Nasturtium *Tropaeolum majus* (page 56)

Prickly pear *Opuntia* spp. (page 58)

Primrose *Oenothera elata* ssp. and *O. speciosa* (page 162)

Radish, wild *Raphanus sativus* (page 60)

Redbud, western *Cercis occidentalis* (page 164)

Sea rocket *Cakile* spp. (page 228)

Sea fig *Carpobrotus chilensis*, *C. edulis* (page 138)

Shepherd's purse *Capsella bursa-pastoris* (page 200)

Sourgrass *Oxalis pes-caprae* (page 202)

Speedwell, water *Veronica anagallis-aquatica* (page 218)

Strawberry, wild *Fragaria vesca* (page 118)

Violet *Viola* spp. (page 170)

Watercress *Nasturtium officinale* (page 220)

CALIFORNIA GOLDEN CURRANT

PROTECTING YOURSELF

Foraging is hardly a dangerous endeavor, but that does not mean it is not without risk. Every forager faces three distinct types of risk: digestive, physical, and legal.

- Packing an abundance of goodness into this guide. Berries and seeds, flowers, and roots are some of the edibles included, as well as kelp, crawfish, and even snails (they are delicious).
- Providing multiple pathways to identification. We want to make sure you have success. Foraging *Southern California* provides detailed descriptions, full-page photographs, and comparisons of look-alike species (poisonous or not).
- Lastly—and importantly—providing all the information on poisonous and look-alike species. This guide goes to great lengths to ensure your personal safety.

So take a walk, jump on a bike, or head to the beach; any activity provides an opportunity to nourish yourself with the natural bounty of Southern California. Foraging for these species can improve your health, change your outlook, and even help our environment.

NOTES

Southern California is defined as everything south and east of Santa Barbara. This includes the Channel Islands, the southern part of the Sierra Nevada Mountains, and the Mojave and Sonoran Deserts. Practically speaking, a majority of the species in this guide can be found throughout California. This book focuses on plants that follow people, and humans are everywhere.

Additionally, only four of Southern California's eight islands are included. The other four are either too remote or have restricted access. The islands included are Catalina, Santa Cruz, Santa Rosa, and San Miguel. The islands not listed are San Clemente, Santa Barbara, San Nicolas, and Anacapa.

The maps were produced via a great deal of personal experience and by cross-referencing with two primary sources: CalFlora, a nonprofit that catalogs and maps California's native and invasive plants (calflora.org), and *Sunset Western Gardening Book* (Oxmoor House, 2012). With that said, the range maps are necessarily approximate, as the data sources for some species range from sketchy to nonexistent at times.

Introduction

This book started out as a love affair, morphed into a tragedy, and eventually (and luckily), evolved into a hopeful story.

Foraging is fantastic fun. It is a whimsical delight best shared with others. And that is the genesis of this book—outdoorsy fun with family and friends. The story turned tragic when I realized that many of the plants I would have harvested and recommended just a decade ago should no longer be foraged. Like many other native plants, their numbers are dwindling, and they are losing their competitive advantage amid a changing and challenging environment.

California's natural environment is in peril. While we lead the nation in enterprise and economy, we also lead in the number of extinct, endangered, and threatened aquatic and terrestrial plants and animals.

But there may be a glimmer of hope: Maybe we can graze ourselves to a better future. We just need to rely more heavily on the nature that we create—we need to eat the weeds. By foraging with this guide, you might be able to help.

Eating the weeds isn't just good for our region's ecological health, it is absolutely great for your personal health. Many of the species are superfoods with an impressive nutritional content, boasting many health benefits.

This book lists 118 species in Southern California. A majority of the plants and animals in this book are non-native and thrive and thrive because of human influence. Consuming these species might reduce some of the pressure on native species. While there are native plants in this guide, all are widespread and cosmopolitan (as easily found in the wild as in a residential landscape).

Foraging Southern California has been designed to engage and inspire first-time and intermediate foragers. It does this by:

- Organizing the species by harvestable quality. You shouldn't have to read an entire book for a salad. A goal of this book is to quickly lead you to what you need to know.

TOP 10 EDIBLES

These are the plants to forage for on a daily basis. You can pick these on your way to work or on the hiking path; these are the ones to share with family and friends. They are found in urban areas, wild areas, and all of the areas that sit between those two.

Nearly every part of these plants are consumable—the roots, stalks, leaves, flower buds, flowers, seedpods, fruit, and seeds may all be edible.

CATTAIL
(Typha spp.)

WILD

TYPE: Perennial
STATUS: Native and non-native
LEAF ARRANGEMENT: Bunching sheath
HARVEST TIME: Year-round

HABITAT: Cattail is found in slow-moving fresh water throughout Southern California; it's found next to beaches, in the mountains, and well into the deserts. Marshes and streams, ponds, and catchment basins may host it, or be entirely choked with it. Because of cattail's tolerance for salt, it is also often found in estuaries and irrigation canals. Three varieties of cattail grow in Southern California; one is a non-native (narrowleaf; *Typha angustifolia*), although it is not widespread.

GROWTH: Cattail's height distinguishes it from other reedy, aquatic plants. Its stalks grow 3–13 feet tall. It acts much like a grass, spreading by rhizomes and seeds. Cattails crowd and colonize. Its most distinguishing trait is its flower, which resembles a sausage.

LEAVES: Cattail leaves are long, tough, and fibrous; they are a rich green and sheathed around the stems. While only 0.5–1.5 inches wide, these flat leaves extend out up to 10 feet long.

FLOWERS: The flower of cattail looks like a sausage on a stick. It is wind-pollinated. The top half of the sausage is male and produces fine yellow, tasty pollen; the bottom half is female. It is green, turning to brown, and eventually the site of cottony tuft; this mass catches the wind and spreads its seeds. The two native cattail species bloom May through June; the non-native species blooms March through August.

SEASON: Rhizomes are edible year-round. Harvest flower stalks in spring, flowers and pollen in early summer, and seeds summer through early fall.

BENEFITS: The thick fibrous root (crown and rhizomes) are loaded with starch, fiber, and minerals and nutrients. They've been eaten for millennia.

OTHER NAMES: Narrowleaf and broadleaf cattail.

bulrush   western blue flag

COMPARABLE SPECIES: Luckily, a majority of the other water-bound reedy plants, such as bulrush (page 212), are just as edible. The exception is the western blue flag (*Iris missouriensis*). This water iris's leaves rarely get taller than 18 inches. Western blue flag is typically found above 3,800 feet and is most common in the San Bernardino Mountains and around Big Bear Lake. The roots and rhizomes are poisonous to eat and can be an irritant when touched.

NOTES: Cattail is the perfect plant to forage in urban areas. Nearly all of it is edible: the underwater roots, the crown, the young stalks, the green and immature flowers, and even the pollen and the tiny seeds. Its leaves and stalks are used to make everything from sandals and placemats to flooring and emergency shelters. It is sometimes so abundant that foraging it helps improves the area's ecological health. However, never harvest from waters that get outfall from urban areas—the metals and toxins that stream off are pulled from the water by plants like cattail.

CHEESEWEED
(Malva parviflora)

WILD

TYPE: Annual
STATUS: Non-native
LEAF ARRANGEMENT: Alternate; leaves are round
HARVEST TIME: Spring is best, but anytime the plant is present

HABITAT: Cheeseweed is a people-follower and can be found in nearly every urban neighborhood, including mountain and desert communities. It prefers dry, disturbed soils. Look for it at trailheads, along the sunny sides of buildings, and anywhere recently disturbed. It is not found in the wilds of the desert.

GROWTH: This annual grows to nearly 3 feet tall and wide. While the base of the plant can get woody with age, most of the plant is fleshy and supple. Its distinguishing characteristics are its ample growth and its round leaves, which are a deeply rich green.

LEAVES: Always facing the sun (phototropic), the leaves are round, slightly lobed, and have serrated edges. They are 1–4 inches wide, sit atop a long stem (petiole), and are a rich, deep green.

FLOWERS: The small flowers have 5 petals and can be lilac, pink, white, or even slightly blue. Flowers are found at the axis between the petiole and stalk. They bloom from March to October.

FRUIT: Cheeseweed gets its name from its fruit, which resembles a cheese wheel. The fruit is disk-like and about 0.25 inch wide.

SEASON: For the best-tasting greens, harvest in winter and early spring. However, the leaves and fruits can be harvested anytime it is found, which is nearly year-round in some parts of Southern California.

BENEFITS: Cheeseweed is a superfood. It is rich in chlorophyll, calcium, fiber, iron, magnesium, pectin, potassium, selenium, and vitamins A and C. It also has many health benefits: its leaves, shoots, and roots are anti-inflammatory and contain antioxidants; they also help reduce the severity of coughs, can help clear lungs, and, thanks to their alkaline nature, can help settle acidic stomachs.

OTHER NAMES: Mallow

geranium   ivy geranium   hollyhock

COMPARABLE SPECIES: Both common geranium and ivy geranium (*Pelargonium* spp.) might be confused with cheeseweed, and both will upset your stomach if eaten. The leaves of *Pelargonium* species may have stripes or colors, and all leaves have a distinct scent when crushed. Cheeseweed does not have a strong smell. Hollyhock (*Alcea rosea*, page 156) is also often confused with cheeseweed. If you make that mistake, do not worry. Hollyhock is from the mallow family and is edible.

NOTES: Leaves are eaten raw, boiled, or roasted, but its bland flavor and hairy texture means it is best prepared with many other greens and flavors. The fruits can be eaten raw and are delicious. Nibble on the immature green fruits whenever you find them. They are nutty and quench thirst.

DANDELION
(Taraxacum spp.)

WILD

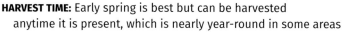

TYPE: Perennial
STATUS: Non-native
LEAF ARRANGEMENT: Basal rosette
HARVEST TIME: Early spring is best but can be harvested
  anytime it is present, which is nearly year-round in some areas

HABITAT: Dandelion is a people-follower and thrives off of our impact on the land. It prefers moist, slightly acidic, and compacted soils. It does as well in shade as sun. It is fairly easy to find around urban areas but is not as prevalent in the more remote areas of Southern California. It is also easier to find west of the mountains than in the desert.

GROWTH: There are 3 varieties of the common perennial dandelion weed: *Taraxacum erythrospermum, T. officinale,* and *T. officinale vulgare.* All are low growing and rarely more than 4 inches high and 8 inches wide.

LEAVES: Dandelion leaves look like that of healthy lettuce: deep rich green without a hairy or rough texture. There is some variation between leaves. All are shaped like an elongated paddle and are wider towards the end. Some leaves may be lobed or lightly or deeply toothed. Leaf size is 1.5–4 inches long and 0.5–1 inch wide.

FLOWERS: Some dandelions only flower in winter; others bloom intermittently throughout the year. A striking yellow composite flower about 1 inch wide proudly stands 3–12 inches above the leaves. The petals are edible.

ROOTS: The taproot (peeled, dried, and roasted) makes an excellent, healthy tea that is reputed to purify the liver and stimulate the gallbladder. Dandelion has a large taproot, which tastes like healthy dirt.

SEASON: Spring is its most abundant season and provides the best-tasting leaves, but the plant can, and should, be eaten anytime it is spotted. In some areas it can be found year-round.

BENEFITS: Dandelion leaves are a superfood. They are loaded with calcium; essential fatty acids; iron; magnesium; phosphorus; potassium; sodium; and vitamins A, B, and C. The entire plant has both anti-inflammatory and antioxidant qualities. Dandelion can also help reduce acne and skin rashes.

OTHER NAMES: Common dandelion, red-seeded dandelion

cat's ear   chicory   hedge mustard   sheep sorrel   shepherd's purse   sow thistle

COMPARABLE SPECIES: The plants that most resemble dandelion are also edible. These include cat's ear, young chicory (page 196), hedge mustard, sheep sorrel (page 86), shepherd's purse (page 200), and sow thistle (page 88).

NOTES: Dig in—dandelion is easy to find. The leaves taste like muted spinach, although older leaves are bitter. The entire plant is edible: leaves, stems, flowers, and roots. The leaves, stems, and flowers are eaten raw or lightly steamed.

FENNEL, SWEET
(Foeniculum vulgare)

WILD

TYPE: Perennial roots, but the plant dies back every year

STATUS: Non-native

LEAF ARRANGEMENT: Basal rosette

HARVEST TIME: Young leaves are best in spring; harvest flowers in late spring and seeds in summer.

HABITAT: Definitely a people-follower, fennel is abundant west of the mountains. It prefers dry and disturbed soils and is not deterred by salt, whether from ocean exposure, overgrazing, or reclaimed water. It can be found along roads, busy trails, next to paved surfaces, and anywhere humans have disturbed the landscape.

GROWTH: Fennel starts growing in January as a small clump, and by late spring/early summer it can produce flower stalks more than 6 feet tall. The plant can be over 2 feet wide. The hollow, strong flower stalks shoot well above the plant and support an abundance of yellow flowers on top. Mature plants have swollen bulbs at their base. Its distinguishing attribute is its strong anise- or licorice-like fragrance.

LEAVES: With leaves that look like large, light-green feathers, it resembles a fern when young. The leaves grow on stems that get 18 inches long and are finely dissected in linear divisions. The leaves look a lot like dill, but dill's leaves are thicker.

FLOWERS: An abundance of tiny, pale yellow flowers sit atop strong stalks that have a powdery, bluish waxy coating. The flowers are huge landing pads for large pollinators and look like umbrellas (they are technically known as umbels). It blooms May through September.

SEASON: Young leaves are best in spring; harvest flowers in late spring and seeds in summer and early fall.

BENEFITS: Fennel is considered a superfood. It is an excellent source of vitamin C. It is a very good source of copper, fiber, folate, manganese, phosphorus, and potassium. And it is a source of calcium, iron, magnesium, and vitamin B3. The plant has anti-inflammatory and antioxidant qualities, and its fibrous nature has benefits for the digestive system and can help alleviate stomach upset.

OTHER NAMES: Biscuit root, sweet fennel, and anise

fern   poison hemlock

COMPARABLE SPECIES: With its strong licorice-like smell, fennel is difficult to confuse with any other plant. However, its leaves can be confused with those of ferns (page 204) and members of the carrot/parsley family, most notably poison hemlock (page 28). Always crush a leaf and smell it before consuming fennel.

NOTES: Young leaves, stems, bulb, and seeds are edible. All can be eaten raw, added to dishes, or lightly cooked, boiled, or steamed. Graze on any part of this plant all day. It is good for you, refreshing, and freshens your breath. It has a strong licorice-like flavor.

FILAREE, RED-STEMMED
(Erodium cicutarium)

TYPE: Low-growing annual
STATUS: Non-native
LEAF ARRANGEMENT: Opposite and pinnately compound
HARVEST TIME: Late winter through early summer

WILD

HABITAT: Most anywhere in Southern California, although it becomes noticeably sparse in the low desert. Filaree prefers dry soils, and its presence indicates that the soil is compacted. Look for it around trail-heads, well-traveled paths, and around buildings in public parks. It is also a common garden weed.

GROWTH: In full sun and if little water is present, this fleshy annual will grow no more than 2 inches tall and 6 inches wide. In shade and with more moisture, filaree can grow to 9 inches tall and wide. The hairy red-dish stems, which bear the leaves and flowers, grow from hairy reddish stalks that radiate from an almost-woody clump. The flower evolves into a long narrow seedpod that is shaped like the bill of a stork.

LEAVES: The small, lacy, pinnately lobed leaves have a compound arrangement on the thin stem.

FLOWERS: Filaree produces small light pink to purplish flowers at the ends of its stems that are 2–12 inches tall and erect. These flowers have 5 petals and are no bigger than 0.25 inch across. The center of the flower is a dark purple.

SEASON: Spring is the best time to find moist and easily digestible leaves, but filaree can be harvested anytime it is found.

BENEFITS: Filaree is tasty and nutritious, although it is not considered a superfood. It contains vital nutrients, vitamins, fiber, and is high in tannins. Filaree also has antioxidant qualities. The root can be chewed like gum.

OTHER NAMES: Coastal heron's bill, clocks, pin grass, pinweed, redstem stork's bill

poison hemlock

feverfew

tansy

COMPARABLE SPECIES: Some members of the carrot/parsley family resemble filaree, most notably poison hemlock (page 28). None of the look-alike plants have hairy stems, all are taller, and their flowers are borne in dense clusters on a long stem arranged like an umbrella. Other similar-looking plants include feverfew and tansy (*Tanacetum* spp.), which both have similar leaves. However, both grow taller than filaree, and they either have yellow flowers, or white flowers with yellow centers. The hairy stem is the key to avoiding trouble.

NOTES: Filaree is mostly harvested for its leaves, although the entire plant is edible. Its leaves taste like parsley. The plant is abundant, making filaree a staple of foraging. Leaves are eaten raw or cooked, much like spinach.

Goosefoot

LAMBSQUARTERS
AND **GOOSEFOOT**
(Chenopodium album and Chenopodium murale)

WILD ORNAMENTAL

TYPE: Annual
STATUS: Non-native
LEAF ARRANGEMENT: Alternate, arrowhead-shaped
leaves with wavy, toothed margins
HARVEST TIME: Best in spring, but can be harvested anytime

HABITAT: Lambsquarters and goosefoot can be found nearly everywhere in Southern California, although they are more abundant within 125 miles of the coast. In the desert they are more common in areas with monsoons. They tolerate salty soil and often grow alongside grazing animals, in agricultural areas, and in coastal gardens.

GROWTH: These two plants are nearly identical and both vary in height and range from 6 inches up to 3.5 feet, and they reach 9–18 inches wide. The stalks and stems become reddish with age. The difference between these two is leaf color; lambsquarters's leaves are paler and grayer.

LEAVES: Arrowhead-shaped leaves with wavy edges that are slightly toothed. Leaves are arranged opposite of each other on small stems off a stalk and 0.75–1.5 inches long. When young, lambsquarters's leaves are whitish green, as if it they were dusted with a fine powder. Mature leaves are a pale bluish or yellowish green. Goosefoot's leaves are a darker rich green.

FLOWERS: Self-pollinated (or pollinated by the wind), they do not have showy flowers. The flower stems, radiating from the top of a stalk, are comprised of tiny green sticky balls. *C. album* blooms June through October; *C. murale* blooms nearly all year.

SEASON: While spring is the best time to find tasty greens, it can be eaten anytime it's found, which is nearly year-round along the coast. Late summer and early fall are the best times to harvest seeds.

BENEFITS: Ancestors of spinach, these plants have been eaten for centuries all over the world. They contain high amounts of calcium, manganese, and vitamins A and C, along with vitamin B6, protein, and riboflavin.

OTHER NAMES: White goosefoot, nettle leaf goosefoot, green goosefoot

brittlebush   nightshade   amaranth   pigweed

COMPARABLE SPECIES: The leaf could be confused with three other plants. Brittlebush (*Encelia* spp.) looks similar when young. The difference is in the smell of the leaves: brittlebush is full of resins and smells awful. Nightshade (white and Douglas', page 114) also has a similarly shaped leaf and is toxic if uncooked. The difference is that the nightshades' leaves are smoother around the edges and it has pretty, nearly ever-blooming flowers. And lastly, lambsquarters resembles amaranth and pigweed, which are in the same family as goosefoot and highly nutritious.

NOTES: Leaves are eaten raw or cooked. The seeds are also edible.

MUSTARD
(Brassica spp.*)*

WILD

TYPE: Semi-woody fleshy annual

STATUS: Non-native

LEAF ARRANGEMENT: Basal growth when young; alternate when on a stalk

HARVEST TIME: From the first rain until the area dries out: typically midsummer

HABITAT: Mustard is a car-follower and can be found nearly everywhere. The taller varieties, like black mustard (*Brassica nigra*), are found closer to the ocean; the lower-growing varieties, such as common mustard (*Brassica tournefortii*) are found in the desert.

GROWTH: Mustard's rich deep green leaves, tall flower spikes, and pungent smell make identification easy—tear a leaf, take a whiff, and if it smells like mustard, then it is. The stalks of mustard grow between 1 and 5 feet tall. This group of plants includes one of California's most iconic weeds: black mustard.

LEAVES: Mustard leaves vary greatly, even on a single plant. Leaves of an emerging plant form at its base and are large, oblong, and deeply lobed and slightly serrated. As the stalk grows, leaves become narrower and toothed, with some leaves having smooth edges, while others are slightly serrated.

FLOWERS: The bright yellow flowers grow from short stems that are whorled around a central stalk (raceme). The stems get shorter as the stalk gets taller. Each small flower has four petals. Most bloom from March to August.

SEEDS PODS: Seeds are about 1 inch long, needle-like, and typically point upwards.

SEASON: Found from November to when the plants start dying back, which might be as late as September. Younger leaves are easier to chew and enjoy; older leaves are fibrous and tough (but no less beneficial).

BENEFITS: Mustard is a superfood. Very high in fiber and vitamins A, C, and K, it's also high in calcium, folate, iron, manganese, potassium, and vitamins B6 and E. And it has some fatty acids, protein, and phosphorus. It helps reduce inflammation, promotes liver health, lowers cholesterol, and aids in bone building. Its seeds and flowers are also edible.

OTHER NAMES: Black mustard, Mediterranean cabbage, rapeseed

| yellow rocket | wallflower | hedge mustard | London rocket |

COMPARABLE SPECIES: Many plants have flowers that look similar. These include yellow rocket (*Barbarea* spp.), wallflower (*Erysimum* spp.), hedge mustard (*Sisymbrium officinale*), and London rocket (*Sisymbrium* spp., page 72). The leaves of yellow rocket and hedge mustard look somewhat similar too. The best way to identify it is to tear a leaf and smell it—only mustard has that distinct mustard smell.

NOTES: You can eat the leaves raw or cooked. It is healthiest to pick the lower leaves. Young plants are more palatable than older specimens. Every member of Brassica is edible.

NASTURTIUM
(Tropaeolum majus)

WILD ORNAMENTAL

TYPE: Fleshy sprawling perennial, but an annual in areas of drought or that freeze
STATUS: Non-native
LEAF ARRANGEMENT: Alternate and orbicular
HARVEST TIME: Year-round

HABITAT: Climbing and tumbling up and over all types of terrain, nasturtium is easy to find along the coast and in many inland urban areas. A people-follower, it prefers semi-shade, some humidity, seasonal rainfall, and, preferably, temperatures above freezing. You will not find nasturtium in the desert or the high mountains.

GROWTH: Nasturtium can overrun shaded moist environments, blanketing ground cover, scrambling over shrubs, and climbing trees. Its most distinguishing characteristic is its fleshy nature—no matter how big the vining plant gets, it always remains supple and succulent.

LEAVES: New leaves are heart-shaped and lobed; older leaves are round and no more than 5 inches across. Leaf color ranges from deep green to a pale yellowish green. Leaves dangle from long stems attached to a sprawling stalk. The leaf is attached to the stem in its center, like an umbrella.

FLOWERS: Nasturtium produces funnel-like flowers with five petals; flowers range from vibrant oranges and reds to yellows. The flower has a defining characteristic: a spur grows away from the base, and it can be curved and up to 1 inch long. Nasturtium is almost everblooming, although the peak of its season occurs from March through July.

SEASON: The best time to harvest every part of this plant is from winter through spring, though you can consume anytime it's found. It can be found year-round in some coastal and protected urban communities.

BENEFITS: The primary benefit of nasturtium is that you can eat the entire plant. It contains fiber and many nutrients and vitamins and also has antioxidant qualities. Its flowers are high in vitamin C.

OTHER NAMES: No other names

COMPARABLE SPECIES: Because of its fleshy nature, dynamic flowers, and vining habit, there is no species that acts or looks like nasturtium.

NOTES: Leaves and stems are eaten raw or cooked. The leaves have a deep horseradish flavor and are best mixed with other greens or added to other dishes, such as eggs or stews. The stems have only a hint of horseradish.

PRICKLY PEAR
(*Opuntia* spp.)

WILD

TYPE: Shrub with succulent stems
STATUS: Mostly native
LEAF ARRANGEMENT: Succulent
HARVEST TIME: Winter and spring for young pads; harvest fruit in summer and fall

WARNING: The fine hair-like spines are hard to spot—be careful when eating!

HABITAT: Prickly pears are a large group of mostly native cactus species that live alongside humans. They are found everywhere in Southern California except for the low desert. The grizzlybear prickly pear can even be found at elevations as high as 8,000 feet. While a majority of *Opuntia* species prefer areas that receive 6 inches or more of rainfall per year, beavertail prickly pear can be found growing in areas with just 4 inches. *O. ficus-indica*, a non-native and found along the coast, is the species most likely sold in grocery stores.

GROWTH: Some varieties only grow to 2 feet tall, while others reach up to 15 feet tall and just as wide. The plant is prone to breakage, which enables the plant to spread: when a pad touches soil, it roots.

LEAVES: Resembling paddles, the leaves are oval, flat, and thick. They range from 8 to nearly 24 inches long and 4 to 16 inches wide. Older plants are green to bluish green; young pads are a much lighter green. Pads have both long sturdy spines more than an inch in length and tiny hair-like spines (glochids) that readily embed in skin.

FLOWERS: Cup-shaped and 2–3 inches in diameter, flowers range in color from pale yellow and orange yellow to orangish red and neon pink.

FRUIT: This is one of the sweetest and most abundant native fruits in Southern California. They are 1–5 inches in length and 1–3 inches wide. A majority of the fruits (known as tunas) have tiny hair-like spines that must be carefully avoided.

SEASON: Young pads are found in winter and spring; summer and fall are the best times to harvest the fruit.

BENEFITS: Pads are high in calcium, fiber, potassium, and vitamins A and C, and have antioxidant properties. The mucus-like sap can be used to treat skin ailments, such as sunburn.

OTHER NAMES: Nopal, pancake cactus, beavertail cactus

COMPARABLE SPECIES: There are no comparable species.

NOTES: All *Opuntias* are edible. The pads (nopales), flowers, and fruit (tunas) are eaten raw or cooked. While young pads taste best and are easiest to prepare, older pads can be eaten, too, but only the pulpy interior. Boiling or cooking the pads reduces the mucus-like sap.

RADISH, WILD
(Raphanus sativus)

WILD

TYPE: Annual/biennial

STATUS: Non-native

LEAF ARRANGEMENT: Basal growth when young; alternate leaf arrangement when on a stalk

HARVEST TIME: Midwinter to mid-spring

HABITAT: Wild radish is a definite people-follower. It prefers dry, disturbed, shallow soils, and you'll find it in the margins of campsites, along busy trails, and in the undeveloped areas in and around cities. It is far more prevalent west of the mountains.

GROWTH: The plant's rich green leaves and tall, slender flower spikes of pastel blooms make this biennial easy to identify. The stalks of wild radish grow between 1 and 5 feet tall and can eventually grow to 2 feet wide. Wild radish belongs to the mustard family and shares many of mustard's attributes.

LEAVES: The end of a wild radish leaf is broadly shaped, like a paddle; the rest of the leaf is broken into lobed segments, with smaller segments closer to the stem. The leaf has a smoother texture than that of a mustard leaf.

FLOWERS: Found on tall stalks that radiate in all directions, the flowers of wild radish can range from pale white or yellow to lilac. The flower has four petals and blooms February to July.

SEASON: Leaves are best harvested in late winter and early spring, although they can be eaten anytime. Flowers are eaten in spring, seedpods spring through midsummer, and roots are best in fall.

SEEDS: The seedpods of wild radish are round and look like bean pods, but they have a pointy end and typically grow towards the sun, not downward.

BENEFITS: The leaves and roots are high in fiber and vitamin C and improve digestive health. The radish's seeds are a stimulant, raw or brewed.

OTHER NAMES: No other names

bittercress   London rocket   mustard   shepherd's purse

COMPARABLE SPECIES: Luckily, the plants that resemble wild radish are all edible. These include bittercress, London rocket (page 72), mustard (page 54), and shepherd's purse (page 200). The primary way to distinguish between wild radish and such look-alikes is to note the radish's smooth leaf texture and its pastel blooms.

NOTES: Wild radish is an excellent source of fiber, and the entirety of the plant is edible: leaves, stems, flowers, seeds, crown, and roots. Naturally, the younger it is, the more palatable it is. Young leaves can be eaten raw, with older leaves lightly cooked. The bulbous crown is eaten raw when young, chopped and cooked when older. Flowers and green seedpods are eaten raw.

LONDON ROCKET

Digestive Risk

Foraging involves eating wild foods from unfamiliar lands. Naturally, there are risks with such an enterprise. Below are six risks you face when eating foraged food.

MISIDENTIFICATION: While there are far more edible plants than not, this book goes to great lengths to help you identify those that are edible and avoid those that are toxic or inedible, including a chapter dedicated to Southern California's most poisonous plants. Every foraging recommendation features a thorough description of the plant's physical attributes, and every recommendation also includes common look-alikes—and how to tell them apart. Only consume a plant if you're certain you've identified it correctly. When in doubt, throw it out.

PATHOGENS: Digesting a pathogen is the greatest threat to a forager's health. Below are steps to reduce this hazard.

Look for Signs: Materials that are discolored; misshapen; or have a rancid, bitter, or unpleasant smell are warning signs not to forage. Trust your sense of smell and your gut instinct.

Be Aware of Wildlife: Foraging around livestock, areas with a lot of wildlife (such as wetlands), or urban areas with dogs increases the risk of disease. Always wash and cook your harvest if picked from environments like these.

Avoid the Dirt: Pathogens love soil, and the closer you harvest to it, the more risk you have. If there is a choice between a specimen that's low to the ground or one that's high up, choose the one that's higher up.

Wash Your Harvest: Always wash your haul in water that is much warmer than the harvest. The positive temperature difference creates a pressure differential that should help pull pathogens and toxins out, instead of sucking them in.

Cook It: If you have even the slightest doubt about pathogens—cook your harvest. Whether boiled, roasted, or steamed, the goal is for the thickest part to reach at least 165 degrees.

FOOD ALLERGIES: If it is your first time eating a particular foraged food, take a few small bites only. Wait a couple hours to see if anything happens, and if not, dig in. With the exception of some nuts, a majority of this book's recommendations should not produce an allergic reaction in most people.

FOREIGN BODIES: When you harvest from the wild, you'll bring home wild things. Make it a habit to allow your harvest to sit for 20 minutes before washing it. This time allows insects the opportunity to flee. If you suspect your find could harbor an insect that has bored into the plant—this isn't uncommon with flowers, fruits, and seeds, then always cook before eating.

METALS: Our transportation system pollutes the environment a great deal. While it is transportation's gaseous pollutants, especially nitrous oxides, that create the conditions that enable most of the invasive plants in this book to thrive, it is particulate pollutants that pose the greatest risk to urban foragers. Urban soils can be much higher in potentially dangerous metals than native soils. These metals include antimony, copper, lead, mercury, nickel, and zinc. In elevated doses, some of these metals are neurotoxins, whereas others are carcinogens. To limit your exposure, avoid foraging along roads and around commercial areas.

HERBICIDES: Avoid collecting in areas treated with herbicides, as they've been linked to a number of health concerns. An area or plant treated with a herbicide will sit in contrast to an untreated area nearby. Look for straight lines, which contrast with nature's natural, wilder growth patterns. Look for islands, strips or areas of dead material, or areas where only one type of plant is dead or injured, such as all grasses or broadleaf plants. Also look for changes in soil color or texture. If any of these contrasts with the surrounding landscape, it might be an indication of herbicides and toxins.

General Signs of Plants to Avoid
- Strips, patches, and other organized areas of dead vegetation
- Shriveled leaves and stems isolated to only certain areas
- Purple leaves in only certain areas
- Yellow spots on leaves or plants in certain areas

- Areas where only one type of plant is dead, such as grasses or broadleaf plants, which indicates a selective herbicide
- Plants that look mottled or don't seem to have produced enough chlorophyll (chlorosis)
- Soils that look different—they may have a waxy or glossy look, be richer or deeper in color, and/or may have small puddles of water or the signs of puddles (residue rings)

Physical Risk

The natural environment is rife with physical risk. Thorns and irritants, tripping hazards, and rogue waves are a natural part of our outdoor pursuits. Follow the tips below.

CLOTHING: Long pants, ankle-high boots, long-sleeve shirts, a sun hat, sunglasses, and gloves will help ensure your comfort and safety. And if you are in the mountains, be sure to bring mosquito repellent.

DRESS LIKE A FLOWER: Do not blend into the environment. Just the opposite—give animals large and small the opportunity to scurry away. Make sure you are seen and heard. As a bonus, bees do not see light colors as a threat, and you are less likely to be harassed if you're wearing pastels or white.

DO NOT TOUCH YOUR FACE: Whether it's because of irritating milky sap, nearly invisible spines, or the oil from poison oak, seasoned foragers never touch their face unless they have thoroughly cleaned their hands.

BE AWARE: Whether it's stumbling into blackberry or mesquite, getting slapped by a wave, or twisting an ankle in shin-deep mud, most accidents happen because of inattention. Breathe deeply, be patient, and always place yourself in your surroundings—be aware of your intentions, movement, and physical environment.

RATTLESNAKES: All of Southern California is rattlesnake country. There are seven species and several subspecies in the state. Rattlers can be identified by their triangular head and blotches on their skin. Not all have rattles. Rattlesnakes absolutely do not want a confrontation—give them advanced warning (stomp on the ground when walking), do not approach them, and always allow them time for a slow retreat. You are likely to see them on trails when the temperatures range from the mid-70s to mid-80s.

COUGARS: The carnivorous cougars are the top of the food chain in the wilds of Southern California. They live in the foothills and mountains throughout the region. But finding a paw print is far more likely than actually seeing one—humans spook them. Making noise is your best defense. Mountain lions mostly hunt at dawn and dusk, so try to avoid hiking alone during those times.

BLACK BEARS: Black bears have learned to live around humans. They live in mountainous areas and can be found from the Los Padres National Forest to the San Jacinto Mountains, though they are a relatively rare sight overall. They are most common in the San Bernardino and San Gabriel Mountains. Your best defense is to make noise—they want to avoid a confrontation.

MEDICINAL USE: Always consult your doctor. Some of the species listed in this book may have medicinal benefits, and some of those benefits may be included. But before using any of these species for medicinal purposes, consult a professional. Also keep in mind that your body's response to any foraged items may be unique.

POISON OAK: Few plants inhabit as many environments as poison oak. If you are foraging within 100 miles of the coast (almost half of the region's width), you have probably encountered poison oak. If you believe that you have brushed against this madly irritating vining shrub, follow these tips:

- Wash your hands with soap and cold water immediately.
- Wash any exposed areas, such as ankles and wrists, as soon as possible.
- Do not touch your clothing.
- If possible, remove your clothing before jumping into your car or walking into your home.

- Wash your clothing without touching anything else.
- Place your shoes in the sun for 2 days.

Legal Risk

Just because nobody is likely to stop you from harvesting a majority of these species, it does not necessarily mean doing so is legal. There are four areas where you may encounter restrictions and/or legal consequences from foraging.

TRESPASSING: Do not enter private land unless you have permission. If caught on private property while foraging, you can be cited for trespassing and/or poaching or theft.

NO COLLECTING ALLOWED: Whether on the inland reaches of Marine Protected Areas (MPAs) or special reserves, state colleges, or commercial property, there are many places that are open to the public but do not allow harvesting. Go online and review restrictions before heading out.

GET A LICENSE: Foraging in and around the water generally requires a fishing license. Even snaring the invasive crayfish requires a license. The exceptions are fishing off public ocean piers and grabbing seaweed above the tide line.

THREATENED OR ENDANGERED SPECIES: It is illegal to harvest or disturb a species that is listed by the state and/or federal governments as being either threatened or endangered. Luckily, most of the species listed in this book are new arrivals to Southern California, and harvesting them may help native species. Furthermore, the native species recommended are widespread and abundant in our area.

POISON OAK

FLOWERS: Beautiful creamy flower spikes (raceme) makes death camas a delight to spot. Flower spikes are often branched and can grow to 16 inches tall. Spikes are covered in tiny star-like flowers that are light yellow, creamy white, or bright white. The flower's center is mustard yellow. They bloom March–July.

OTHER NAMES: Deathcamas; desert, foothill, Fremont's, or meadow death camas

nut grass   blue dicks   wild onion

COMPARABLE SPECIES: Death camas can be confused with many other plants, not all of which are listed in this book. Nut grass (page 198) might be confused with death camas, but it is smaller growing, has triangular stems, and does not produce showy flowers.

Importantly, death camas might be confused with blue dicks and wild onion. While neither is in this book, both have edible bulbs and are commonly foraged. The flowers of both are much different than those of death camas, so only harvest these plants when in bloom.

NOTES: To be safe—avoid all death camas. Every part is poisonous; the bulb is the most toxic.

NASTURTIUM

ALONG THE SHORELINE

Shorelines have it all. Food items with essential minerals and nutrients, protein, and starch are found in abundance along fresh and saltwater environments. Foraging California's waterways is nourishing and rewarding.

Although rich with abundance, shorelines have peril as well. Watery environments can harbor toxins and disease. Here are three rules for harvesting around water:

1. Never forage around waters that get outfall from agricultural, commercial, or urban drainages, as these may contain hydrocarbons, metals, and pesticides.
2. Unless you absolutely trust the water, always cook your harvest to 165 degrees, the pathogen-killing threshold. Giardia (nausea, diarrhea, cramps) is not uncommon to Southern California. Roots should always be boiled, and sometimes twice.

Avoid waters with scum or oily film, that are overrun by algae, or are discolored—all might have toxins.

BULRUSH
(Bolboschoenus spp. and *Schoenoplectus* spp.)*

TYPE: Perennial and grass-like

STATUS: Native

LEAF ARRANGEMENT: Basal and sheathing

HARVEST TIME: Roots are harvested year-round, young shoots are harvested mid-fall through early spring, and pollen can be collected anytime the plant is blooming.

HABITAT: If the water is slow enough and the soil is deep enough, you'll find bulrush along the coast, in the mountains, and in the deserts. Some varieties thrive in brackish water and are found in estuaries and the Salton Sea. While there are many varieties of bulrush, the edible four offered here all once belonged to the *Scirpus* genus.

GROWTH: Bulrush height ranges from 2 to 14 feet. They spread by seed and underground roots and can colonize large areas. All these plants are part of the sedge family, and a majority have distinct edges along their stems. However, *Schoenoplectus acutus* and *S. americanus* have almost-round stems (they sometimes have a side that seems flat).

LEAVES: Sheathing off stems in a basal fashion, the leaves vary in length. Leaf color ranges from yellow-green to forest green. Leaves tend to be V-shaped, folded, or have a ridged midvein.

FLOWERS: Dangling from long stems in small clusters that look like collapsed umbrellas (spikelets), flowers are minute, somewhat bristly, and hay-brown to grayish brown. They are wind-pollinated. The flowers bloom between April and September.

SEASON: Roots are harvested year-round but are tastiest in fall. Young shoots are best mid-fall through early spring. Pollen can be harvested anytime the plant is blooming.

BENEFITS: Packed with starch, minerals, and fiber, bulrush was a staple of indigenous Americans. Young roots contain sugar.

OTHER NAMES: *Bolboschoenus maritimus*, Alkali bulrush, cosmopolitan bulrush; *Schoenoplectus acutus*, Hardstem bulrush, tule; *Schoenoplectus americanus*, Chairmaker's bulrush, hard stem bulrush; *Schoenoplectus californicus*, California bulrush.

cattails   rush

COMPARABLE SPECIES: Cattail (page 42) and rush (*Juncus* spp.) grow in many of the same environments and might be confused with bulrush. The leaves of cattail can be 10 feet long; bulrush leaves are much shorter. Cattail's flower looks like a sausage on a stick, not dangling hay bristles. The rushes have strictly cylindrical stems (no flat edges anywhere) and its flowers are tiny and star-shaped. Rush flowers have petals, while bulrush does not. Cattail is delicious; rush (*Juncus* spp.) is not edible, but it is not toxic, either.

CELERY, WILD
(Apium graveolens)

TYPE: Annual or biennial herb
STATUS: Non-native
LEAF ARRANGEMENT: Basal and trifoliate leaves
HARVEST TIME: Anytime it is found, which might be year-round

HABITAT: Thriving year-round in water, this annual is far more prevalent along the waterways on the western flanks of our mountains. It's not common on the eastern sides of the mountains, but it can be spotted. It is rare in the deserts and at elevations above 4,000 feet. Because of its tolerance for salts, it is often found around streams along the coast. Look for it in the shade.

GROWTH: Looking like the celery found in grocery stores, wild celery grows narrowly but reaches 1.5–4 feet tall. It is entirely fleshy and a pale yellow-green to a rich green. Its most distinguishing attributes are its celery-like smell and cupped and ribbed celery-like stems.

LEAVES: Stalks are long, but leaf stalks range from 1 to 7 inches, each with a group of 3 leaflets (trifoliate). Each leaflet has a stem, is oblong or ovate, and is roughly 1.5 inches long and lobed, if not slightly toothed.

FLOWERS: Dainty and antique-white, celery blooms are beautiful. Arranged in umbrella-like clusters (compound umbel), the total arrangement is 2–6 inches across. Celery blossoms are far more airy than other umbel-producing plants. Each flower is tiny and has 5 petals. It blooms May–July.

SEASON: Anytime it is found, which might be year-round

BENEFITS: Packed with essential minerals and nutrients, and reputed to have anti-inflammatory and antioxidant qualities, celery is nearly a superfood.

OTHER NAMES: Garden celery, smallage

poison hemlock   water hemlock

COMPARABLE SPECIES: There are two highly poisonous plants that have flowers similar to celery's: poison hemlock (page 28) and water hemlock (page 36). Poisonous hemlock is much bigger, sometimes growing to 8 feet, and its leaves have an unpleasant scent when crushed (the scent is not celery-like). Water hemlock's leaves are comprised of lance-like leaflets, not roundish like those of celery. And both the hemlock species have round stems, not cupped and ribbed stems like in celery.

NOTES: Leaves and stalks are eaten raw or cooked. The uppermost growth accumulates nitrates and should be avoided. The flavor is celery-like but far stronger.

MINER'S LETTUCE
(Claytonia perfoliata (and spp.))

TYPE: Annual succulent herb
STATUS: Native
LEAF ARRANGEMENT: Rosette grower
HARVEST TIME: Year-round

HABITAT: This fast-growing annual is common in the waterways within 110 miles of the coast and can be found growing at elevations of up to 7,000 feet. While rare in the desert, it can be found in mountainous environments and protected aquatic areas. It is absent in the low desert. It prefers constant moisture and acidic and semi-dense soils.

GROWTH: Miner's lettuce is instinctively edible. Its moist, roundish, and rich, shiny-green leaves are found in shaded, cool, and moist environments—the perfect treat for the coolest locations. It gets no taller than 8 inches, but it spreads well. Its most distinguishing attribute is its delicate tiny white flowers, which grow on a stem from the center of the leaf.

LEAVES: Miner's lettuce leaves are distinct. Young basal leaves are more lance-like. Older leaves are found on stems and are disk-like, cupped upward, and have unusual pointy flairs on their edges. The stems of older leaves are up to 7 inches long, but they are not upright. These leaves are thick, and their color is a rich forest green.

FLOWERS: Claytonia flowers are dainty. Each leaf will produce a stem that supports 1 to 8 tiny flowers. Each flower is about 0.1 inch wide, has 5 petals, and is starkly translucent white. It flowers February–May.

SEASON: Miner's lettuce can be harvested year-round.

BENEFITS: Miner's lettuce has kept adventurers and pioneers healthy for hundreds of years. The leaves are high in vitamin C and have beneficial amounts of iron and vitamin A.

OTHER NAMES: Claytonia

COMPARABLE SPECIES: With the cupped leaf on spindly stems, and its dainty flower, nothing compares to miner's lettuce.

NOTES: Leaves and stems are mostly eaten raw, but they can be lightly cooked. Leaves are moist, if not gooey, and absolutely refreshing. They are wonderful when added to other greens.

SPEEDWELL, WATER
(Veronica anagallis-aquatica)

TYPE: Perennial herb
STATUS: Non-native
LEAF ARRANGEMENT: Opposite and simple, oblong
HARVEST TIME: Midwinter to mid-spring is best, but anytime it is found

HABITAT: Found within 100 miles of the coast, and along freshwater areas, water speedwell prefers acidic, water-soaked, salt-free soils. It is found in slow-moving streams, ponds, and saturated meadows. It is rare in deserts and estuaries. It is commonly found around watercress.

GROWTH: This fleshy perennial readily spreads by underground stems (rhizomes) and is often found as a low-growing mat. Water speedwell can also grow higher than 2 feet tall and nearly as wide. The stems are round and reddish brown-green, turning rusty red when dry.

LEAVES: Oblong, smooth, and a light to rich green, this perennial's leaves look instinctively edible. They are 1–3 inches long, narrow, and have a pronounced point. Its midvein is indented. Notably, the leaves are opposite and sheathed—there are no leaf stems (petioles).

FLOWERS: Petite, beautiful, and flat, water speedwell's flowers are blue or lightly lavender and have a violet center. They have 4 tiny, yet proud, petals. They bloom in pyramid-like spirals (racemes), although never at once. It blooms May–September.

SEASON: Speedwell grows in earnest when waters recede and the days lengthen: midwinter to mid-spring are the best time for leaves and stems, although it can be harvested anytime found.

BENEFITS: Along with the chlorophyll and fiber, the leaves are also high vitamin C.

OTHER NAMES: No other names

cardinal flower

COMPARABLE SPECIES: The plant that most resembles water speedwell, and grows in the same environments, is cardinal flower (*Lobelia cardinalis*). It has long, smooth, and oblong leaves, and a similar flowering structure (raceme). However, its leaves are alternate and have short stems. Its flowers are scarlet red and long-throated. *Lobelia* is not edible, but it will not hurt you.

NOTES: Leaves and stems are eaten raw or cooked. The flavor is bland and much like chickweed.

CAUTION: If you suspect pathogens are present in the water, which is not unusual in areas with a lot of wildlife, then boil the leaves and stalks before eating. If you suspect heavy metals or pollution in the water, not uncommon along urban drainages, then do not eat them.

WATERCRESS
(Nasturtium officinale)

TYPE: Perennial herb
STATUS: Native
LEAF ARRANGEMENT: Odd-pinnate
HARVEST TIME: Year-round, but late fall through early spring is best

HABITAT: Common in western-facing waterways within 100 miles of the coast, watercress is absent in the low desert, but it might be found in the high desert. It does not grow in fast-moving water, but in shallow pools that may or may not have moving water. Look for it around lakes and slow-moving streams.

GROWTH: Watercress can be a spreading mass of roundish leaves that gets no higher than 10 inches, or a tall mustard-like perennial (the two are related) that grows to 2 feet, and sometimes taller. To identify it, look for its beautiful round or oval leaves and leaflets.

LEAVES: Young basal leaves are plentiful, roundish, and about 1.5 inches in diameter. Older leaves that grow off the stalks are 4–8 inches long and comprised of up to 5 to 13 leaflets (odd-pinnate). Leaflets are oval or round near the base of the stalk but get progressively narrower farther up. Leaflets may be 2 inches long and half as wide. All leaf edges are slightly indented.

FLOWERS: Watercress has mustard-like flowers. Tiny antique-white flowers grow off short stems that are whorled around a central stalk (raceme). These flower stems (petiole) get shorter as the stalk gets taller. Each small flower has 4 miniature petals. It blooms March–September.

SEASON: Leaves are not as tart or peppery before the plant flowers; harvest in late fall through early spring.

BENEFITS: Watercress has carbohydrates and protein and is high in calcium, iron, phosphorus, and vitamins A and C.

OTHER NAMES: None

poison hemlock   water hemlock

COMPARABLE SPECIES: There are two plants that grow in the same environments and might be confused with watercress: poison hemlock (page 28) and water hemlock (page 36). Both are exceptionally poisonous. Luckily, there are many differences between them. Poisonous hemlock is much bigger, sometimes growing to 8 feet; its leaves have an unpleasant scent when crushed (not peppery like watercress); and its flower heads are umbrella-like, not a spiraling spike. Water hemlock's leaves are comprised of lance-like leaflets, not the round or oval leaves of watercress.

NOTES: Leaves and stalks are eaten raw or cooked. Boiling the leaves softens the flavor, which is strongly tart and peppery. The seed is used like pepper.

CAUTION: If you suspect pathogens are present in the water, which is not unusual in areas with a lot of wildlife, then boil the leaves and stalks before eating them. If you suspect heavy metals could be present, which is not uncommon along urban drainages, then do not forage in that area.

CRAYFISH, RED SWAMP
(Procambarus clarkii)

STATUS: Non-native
HARVEST TIME: Year-round

HABITAT: Crayfish are an easy catch in and around urban waterways. They are found in slowing-moving streams, at the edges of lakes, in constructed wetlands, in urban flood channels, and in agricultural drainages. They hide behind rocks, under leaves, and around submerged logs.

DESCRIPTION: They look like tiny lobsters, to which they are related, and are about 6 inches long. They are murky mud-brown to dark red.

SEASON: Crayfish are eaten year-round.

BENEFITS: The crayfish in Southern California are non-native and compete with native species for scarce resources. Eating them provides you with protein and can support native species in urban waterways.

OTHER NAMES: Crawdads, crawfish, poor man's lobster

COMPARABLE SPECIES: None

NOTES: Crayfish are typically boiled, flavored, then eaten. It is important to make sure that every part of the crayfish reaches 165 degrees when cooking—our waters carry disease. Each is tasty and small. Catching them is the trick. You can use a small net or trap, or slowly pull them out with bait. Another way is to place a bucket behind them, prod the area in front of them, and they will reactively flee in reverse.

CAUTION: Agricultural and urban waterways can contain unhealthy amounts of heavy metals and toxins. Luckily, local watershed agencies have information on stream toxins: you just have to ask. Pathogens are also likely in our fresh waters—and proper cooking will eliminate these threats.

LEGALITIES: While there is no limit to the number of crayfish you can catch, you must have a fishing license. They can only be harvested by hand, line and hook, a dip net, or via trap not larger than 3 feet. It is legal to catch them year-round. For details, visit: www.wildlife.ca.gov/regulations

SNAIL, BROWN GARDEN

(Cornu aspersum)

STATUS: Non-native
HARVEST TIME: Year-round, but most prevalent in spring

HABITAT: The brown garden snail is a cosmopolitan species and can be found throughout the world. It prefers moist, shady, and cool environments. They can be found in residential and commercial landscapes, in irrigated pastures, and growing wild along the coast.

DESCRIPTION: About 1 inch in diameter and as tall, the shells of the brown snail have broad brown and yellowish muddy stripes. Its flesh is a light brown. Snails are nocturnal and are more likely to be found from dusk to dawn.

SEASON: Year-round, but most prevalent in spring

BENEFITS: Brown garden snails are not native, and eating them helps protect gardens, natural landscapes, and native species. They are also power-packed with protein and are rich in calcium, iron, magnesium, phosphorus, and zinc. The brown snail has been cultivated and eaten for millennia.

OTHER NAMES: European garden snail.

milk snail

decollate snail

Southern
California
shoulderband
snail

COMPARABLE SPECIES: There are many mollusks in California, with a majority aquatic and native. There are three mollusks (snails) most likely to be found in the same environments as the brown snail. Milk snail (*Otala lacteal*) is non-native and just as edible, but not as prized. Its shell pattern is more distinctly whorled with light colored bands. The decollate snail (*Rumina decollate*) is a predator of snails. They are smaller, darker, and more linear and narrow. They are neither poisonous nor edible. The last is the less frequent Southern California shoulderband (*Helminthoglypta tudiculata*); its flesh is much darker than the brown snail and its shell is reddish to deep brown. Do not eat the native snail.

NOTES: There are many recipes for snails; here is ours: Purge snails of their mucus by submerging them in water with about ½ cup salt and ¼ cup vinegar for 50 snails. Change the solution until the snails stop producing mucus, which takes about 4 hours. Drain, wash in cold water, and cook in temperatures exceeding 165 degrees for 8 minutes. Drain, wash in cold water, and pull the shrunken meat from the shells with a small fork. From there the meat is baked, broiled, sautéed, or smoked with any number of ingredients. The flavor is a bit unremarkable and pleasant.

CAUTION: If you are not completely certain that the land is toxin free—that there are no hydrocarbons, metals, or pesticides—then the snails' intestines must be cleaned. Place the snails in a container with nothing but a source of water for 2 to 3 days; feed them vegetables, leaves, or meals for 1 or 2 days, and then follow the instructions above.

NEW ZEALAND SPINACH
(Tetragonia tetragonioides)

TYPE: Annual/Perennial
STATUS: Non-native
LEAF ARRANGEMENT: Alternate and simple
HARVEST TIME: Spring, although it can be eaten all year

HABITAT: A people-following plant found from Santa Barbara to San Diego, this large annual/perennial is a coastal dune plant and can rarely be found more than 10 miles from the ocean, although wild colonies have been spotted in Riverside and Imperial Valley. It prefers sandy and saline soils. It does not tolerate a freeze.

GROWTH: With awkward, succulent, and rich green growth, this sprawling plant is easy to spot along the coast. It grows up to 2 feet tall and 4 feet wide. It can be found as one small spindly clump or as a colony of plants covering hundreds of square feet. The easy-to-break stems are a yellowish green.

LEAVES: Leaves have an arrowhead-like shape and are 1–3.5 inches long, and their bumpy crystalline surface makes the leaf stand out. Leaf edges are smooth, the veins are distinctly indented, and the leaf's stem (petiole) is about 1 inch long. Leaf color ranges from deep green to yellow-green.

FLOWERS: Tiny flowers grow from the axis of the stems and leaves. It generally pollinates itself. They are no more than 0.06 inch in diameter and a pale yellow. Flowers bloom April through September.

SEASON: This is a warm-season grower and starts growing in early March. Although leaves are best between March and June, it is eaten anytime it's found, which is nearly year-round.

BENEFITS: Like other greens with oxalic acids, New Zealand spinach is best as a supplement to a salad or dishes, but not as the main course. Low in calories, it does have some beta-carotene, potassium, and protein, as well as vitamins A and C.

OTHER NAMES: Sea spinach

lambsquarters   goosefoot

COMPARABLE SPECIES: The plants that most resemble sea spinach are goosefoot and lambsquarters (page 52). However, the margins of their leaves are lightly toothed, unlike those of New Zealand spinach.

NOTES: Leaves are used as a substitute for spinach and are eaten raw or cooked. Older leaves should be boiled, steamed, or added to dishes. All leaves have a bitter flavor, especially late in the season.

SEA ROCKET
(Cakile spp.*)*

TYPE: Annual herb
STATUS: Non-native
LEAF ARRANGEMENT: Basal growth when young, alternate when on a stalk
HARVEST TIME: Winter–spring for leaves, spring–fall for seedpods

HABITAT: This sand-hugging plant thrives along the entire coast. It lives well above the tide line, but not much farther inland than a mile or so. It gulps the moisture and the salt-laden air. Luckily, this plant tolerates humans well.

GROWTH: Fleshy, mounding, or sprawling, and pale green to grass green, this is only one of a handful of plants that grow directly in the sand.

LEAVES: The leaves feel semi-succulent; they are 1–3 inches long and narrow. The leaves of each species differ: The leaves of *C. edentula* are lance-like; the leaves of *C. maritime* are narrow but deeply lobed.

FLOWERS: Nearly ever-blooming, sea rocket rarely puts on a huge show. It is in the mustard family and has small mustard-like flowers, but each flower stalk only has a small number of flowers blooming at a time. Flowers grow off curved stems that are whorled around a central stalk (raceme). Each small flower has 4 petals.

SEEDPODS: About 0.5 inch long and slender, the seedpod of sea rocket is distinct because of its small bulging middle. Seedpods can be found almost year-round.

SEASON: Winter–spring for leaves, and spring–fall for seedpods

BENEFITS: High in Vitamin C, sea rocket also provides the benefits of chlorophyll and fiber.

OTHER NAMES: No other names

seaside heliotrope

COMPARABLE SPECIES: The most common look-like found in the same sandy environments is the edible and native seaside heliotrope (*Heliotropium curassavicum var. oculatum*). The biggest difference is its size and flowers; seaside heliotrope is smaller-growing and has a flower stalk that curls. Its flowers also have five petals, not four like sea rocket.

NOTES: Leaves, stems, and young seedpods are edible. The taste is a zesty, slightly musty mustard. Older plants can be eaten, but it is best to either cook them or add them to other flavors.

Feather Boa   Wrack or Rockweed   Giant Kelp   Sea Lettuce

FEATHER BOA, GIANT KELP, WRACK OR ROCKWEED, AND SEA LETTUCE (GREEN LAVER)

(Egregia menziesii, Macrocystis pyrifera, Fucus spp., and Ulva lactuca)

With an incredible diversity of macroalgae (kelp and seaweed) in California, and all of it edible, naming these aquatic species is academic. Still, it's always nice to explain what you are serving to others.

Sea vegetables are part of the algae family. These macroalgae are divided between brown, green, and red alga. Kelp is a brown algae and is often considered a giant type of macroalgae. It prefers cool, clear, and rocky waters, making it more common along the central and northern coasts. Seaweeds, the other brown, red, and green alga, are more common in Southern California. Toxic algae, a common term in headlines throughout Southern California, refers to microalgae and the impacts they have on marine environments.

THE PARTS OF KELP AND SEAWEED ARE:

Holdfast: The root-like structure anchoring the algae.

Stipe: The branches and stems.

Blade: The leaves.

Below we'll discuss the legal aspects of harvesting macroalgae, a general description of microalgae, safety guidelines, and a rundown of 4 cosmopolitan and delicious species.

The Legalities of Foraging Macroalgae

California's coast has been pillaged for hundreds of years. We lead the nation in number of extinct, endangered, and threatened aquatic species. Luckily, we are on the mend. Commercial endeavors have been curtailed and some of these laws have implications for recreational foragers.

- A fishing license is needed to pick seaweed from the ocean, although you can salvage it above the tide line anytime without a license.

- One person can only gather 10 pounds of total macroalgae a day.

- It is illegal to harvest or disturb eelgrass (*Zostera* species), surf grass (*Phyllospadix* species,) or sea palm (*Postelsia palmaeformis*).

- It is illegal to gather anything from either the ocean or a beach in state or federal conservation areas, marine protected areas (MPAs), and privately managed reserves.

eelgrass   surf grass   sea palm

Importantly, if you are going into the water to harvest, do not pull the plant. Instead cut off only the part you need: Bring a knife or scissors. Always leave the holdfast in place.

General Description

HABITAT: Macroalgae needs sunlight, relatively shallow water, a stable footing, and a good flow of nutrients. They can be found along the entire coast, but they are more likely around rocky cliffs, jagged jetties, piers, or around docks. While sandy beaches exposed to big waves are poor habitats for algae, they can be found washed ashore.

SEASON: Macroalgae grows with light; the succulent tasty new growth occurs late spring through early fall. Naturally, the best time of day to harvest is at low tide.

BENEFITS: All kelp and seaweed are edible. Most are superfoods—they can contain up to 20 times the minerals and vitamins of land plants. They are very high in calcium, iron, magnesium, manganese, selenium, and sodium. They have high amounts of niacin; riboflavin; and vitamins A, C, and K. They have significant amounts of fiber and protein and have some amount of omega-3 fatty acids. Kelp and seaweed support healthy bones, brains, and metabolism.

NOTES: Blades and stipes are eaten raw, dried, or cooked. When dried, they become a highly nutritious salt additive; sprinkled in eggs and yogurt in the morning, on sandwiches in the afternoon, and to soups and meats in the evening.

Safety Guidelines

Gathering the kelp and seaweed that has recently washed onshore is not only the easiest method of foraging, but it is also far less disruptive to the marine habitat. However, this puts you at a greater risk of eating a pathogen.

- Avoid algae that has been pushed above the surf zone.
- Avoid algae with flies and/or white splotches.
- Avoid algae in and around storm drains.
- Trust your nose—it should smell like ocean. Avoid anything sulfurous or sour.
- Always wash salvaged algae with fresh water that is warmer than air temperature.

* And importantly, never turn your back on the ocean, especially on rocky shores. If you're struck by a wave and not expecting it, the outcome can be painful, if not lethal.

Four Common Types of Sea Vegetables

Below are 4 varieties that are cosmopolitan, easy to find, and delicious.

1. Feather Boa *Egregia menziesii*

DESCRIPTION: A brown algae and perennial, feather boa is common and often found washed ashore. It readily dies back in warming waters and pollution (which makes its presence a good indicator of the local water quality). It looks like its name suggests: stipes are 5 feet or longer and covered with hundreds of perpendicular blades that are mostly small and lance-like.

NOTES: Eat the blades, stipes, and buoyancy sacks raw, cooked, or dried.

CAUTION: If harvesting from the ocean, only cut what you need from the growing ends. Never tug on this species, or you may kill it.

2. Giant Kelp *Macrocystis pyrifera*

DESCRIPTION: A brown algae and perennial, giant kelp is abundant and fast growing. It looks like a giant flexible feather floating on the surface. Its central stipe can be 9 feet long and has long lance-like blades that grow along it. It is a pale orange to rusty brown. It is distinguished by its blades that are attached to stipes via small buoyancy sacks that resemble olives.

BEST USES: Eat the stipes and blades raw, cooked, or dried. It is rich tasting and often sweet. Cutting the stipe near the surface of the water does not kill the kelp or harm its chances of reproduction.

3. Wrack or Rockweed *Fucus* spp.

DESCRIPTION: A brown algae and perennial, wrack is plentiful either washed up or on the rocks. Leathery and thick, fronds grow between 4 inches and 1 foot long and are yellow green, olive green, or a deep brown green. Several varieties have small air sacks in the blades (called bladderwracks). Fronds develop from the base, branch out as they grow, and most have notched ends.

BEST USES: Wrack has a strong fishy flavor and is best used as a salt additive to dishes. It is eaten raw, lightly cooked, or dried. It is also sold as a health supplement.

CAUTIONS: Never pull this alga from the ocean—cut what you need.

4. Sea Lettuce (Green Laver) *Ulva lactuca*

DESCRIPTION: A green algae and an annual, people and sea lettuce prefer the same locations: in protected spots away from the wild surf and where there are plenty of firm footings. Look for it around the pilings of docks and piers, in rocky, shallow waters, and in estuaries. In the water it looks like a thin translucent tortilla with torn and wavy edges; out of the water, it looks small, lime green, and slimy.

BEST USES: Tasty, but tough, it needs to be cut into manageable pieces. It is excellent in salads, as well as when dried and used as a flavoring.

CAUTIONS: Sea lettuce grows in urban waters, and not all of our waters are clean (but we are getting there). Harvesting from a harbor mouth might be clean, but deep in the harbor the sea lettuce might be polluted. Know your waters. Also, never pull this alga from the ocean—just cut what you need.

Other Edible Plants Along the Shoreline

FRESH WATER

Cattail *Typha* spp. (page 42)

Fig, common *Ficus carica* (page 130)

Nut grass (yellow and purple) and papyrus *Cyperus esculentus, C. rotundus,* and *C. papyrus* (page 198)

VERY CLOSE TO THE OCEAN

Nasturtium *Tropaeolum majus* (page 56)

Saltbush, big *Atriplex lentiformis* (page 84)

Sea fig *Carpobrotus chilensis, C. edulis* (page 138)

PIER FISHING

(various species)

Pier fishing is one of the more civilized, sustainable, and enjoyable forms of foraging protein in California. Piers attract many edible fish, and foraging them is both relaxing and exhilarating.

Piers are manmade and have ecosystems unique to their structure. The pilings and rocks attract the clinging species such as anemones, barnacles, mussels, seaweed, and worms. The clingers attract the smaller fish, which leads to bigger fish, and so forth. Humans add to the food chain by tossing bait and debris in the water. Piers attract camp-ready meals.

You do not need a California State Fishing License on piers. You can also have two lines in the water per person. And in case you didn't bring gear, pole rental businesses and bait shops are common near piers.

Codes of Conduct for Protecting a Natural Resource

Piers and jetties are unique ecosystems. As such, they can be adversely affected by our behavior and impacts. The guidelines on the next page are aimed at enhancing your experience and that of every person and generation to follow you.

- Take only what you will eat.
- Stick to the smaller fish, those that are lower on the food chain.
- Return fish with care: do not lay the fish down and do not haphazardly toss it; lower it back in with a bucket, if possible.
- Become familiar with rules for fish size, catch limits, and species that you are prohibited to possess.
- Remove and dispose of your monofilament, plastics, and other debris when leaving.

Importantly, using a hook and line to catch crustaceans, such as crab or lobster, is illegal; if caught, crustaceans must be immediately returned to the water. California's regulations can be viewed at www.wildlife.ca.gov/regulations.

PROTECTING ECOLOGICAL HEALTH

Southern California is one-fifth of the state's area yet has almost half of its population—19 million people. The natural environment is assaulted on a daily basis.

This book has been designed to reduce our impact. It recommends only invasive species and widely distributed native plants. But even that is not enough: how we forage is just as important as what we forage. Use the guidelines below to reduce your impact when foraging.

Never pull a plant: Pulling a plant can expose a huge amount of soil, speeding wind and rain erosion, which leads to soil degradation. Cut the plant instead. Kelp and seaweed should never, ever be pulled.

Take a little from a lot: As a general rule, no more than 10 percent of a plant should be harvested at a time. Like a bee, grab a little and move on. Most of these species are abundant, and following this rule is easy.

Follow the Rule of 7: If you do not see 7 other patches of your targeted species, then do not harvest it. Always leave a majority behind for reproduction.

CUT; DO NOT TEAR: The cleaner the cut, the quicker it heals—avoid tearing at plants and rooted seaweed. Instead, use scissors, which are faster and safer.

DRESS LIKE A FLOWER: Do not blend into the environment. Just the opposite, give animals large and small the opportunity to scurry away—make sure you are seen and heard. As a bonus, bees do not see light colors as threatening, and you are less likely to be harassed in pastels and whites.

HARVEST ROOTS WITH SHARP BLADES: Clean cuts can make a big difference in the amount of dieback following an injury. A clean cut will reduce the amount of surface area exposed to pathogens. An old but sharp boning or chef's knife is perfect for harvesting roots.

HARVEST ROOTS IN FALL: It is always better to harvest roots after the plant has seeded, which is generally by fall. No matter how careful, harvesting roots can kill the plant. Harvesting in fall may sow the next crop.

STAY ON THE TRAIL: The bulk of the recommendations in this book can be found along trails—whether in your neighborhood, along the beach, throughout the Transverse Ranges, or in the lowest points of our two deserts. There is simply no need to go bushwhacking when you use this guide.

BE CONSCIOUS OF FIRE: The Western U.S. is fire-prone—Southern California even more so. Always be aware of fire restrictions in your area, obtain a burning permit, always stay nearby and monitor the fire, and always have no less than half a gallon of water or a pile of soil/shovel readily available. For details and permit info, visit CAL FIRE's page: www.readyforwildfire.org.

Helpful Resources and Bibliography

Foraging has been written about and taught for millennia. There are many reliable sources of additional information.

BOOKS

Balls, Edward K. *Early Uses of California Plants.* University of California Press. 1965.

Clarke, Charlotte Bringle. *Edible and Useful Plants of California.* University of California Press. 1977.

Clarke, Oscar F.; Svehla, Danielle; Ballmer, Greg; and Montalvo, Arlee. *Flora of the Santa Ana River and Environs: With References to World Botany.* Heyday. 2007.

Elpel, Thomas J. *Botany in a Day: The Patterns Method of Plant Identification* 6th Edition. Hops Press. 2013.

Lowry, Judith. *California Foraging: 120 Wild and Flavorful Edibles from Evergreen Huckleberries to Wild Ginger.* Timber Press. 2014.

Garcia, Cecilia, and Adams, James D. Jr. *Healing with Medicinal Plants of the West.* Abedus Press. 2012.

Lombard, Kirk. *The Sea Forager's Guide to the Northern California Coast.* Heyday. 2016.

Nyerges, Christopher. *Foraging California: Finding, Identifying, and Preparing Edible Wild Foods in California.* Falcon Guides. 2014.

Reid, Sara; Wishingrad, Van; and McCabe, Stephen. *Plant Uses: California: Native American Uses of California Plants—Ethnobotany.* University of California Santa Cruz Arboretum. 2009.

Sweet, Muriel. *Common Edible and Useful Plants of the West.* Nature-graph Publishers, Inc. 1976.

Timbrook, Jan. *Chumash Ethnobotany: Plant knowledge among the Chumash people of Southern California.* Heyday Books. 2007.

Wiltens, James. *Edible and Poisonous Plants of Northern California.* Wilderness Press. 1999.

WEBSITES

Eat the Weeds: And other things, too, Green Deane (eattheweeds.com)

Calflora, a nonprofit (calflora.org)

Desert Harvesters, a nonprofit, grassroots effort (desertharvesters.org)

Plants For A Future, a nonprofit (pfaf.org)

Glossary

Alternate Leaves: Leaves that are staggered on a stem and do not align evenly; these contrast with leaves that are located opposite of each other.

Annual: A plant that completes its entire life cycle in a year or less.

Basal: A system of growth where new leaves come from the lowest point. This type of growth often creates a circular pattern, as seen with dandelions, fennel, and wild celery.

Biennial: A plant that completes its entire life cycle within 2 years; it produces vegetative growth in the first year, and fruits in the second year..

Blade: The flattened part of a leaf, or the term for a leaf of seaweed.

Bulb: Underground storage structures that produce roots and shoots.

Chlorophyll: Green pigments produced by plants and some algae that turn the sun's radiant energy into a chemical energy by means of photosynthesis.

Compound Leaf: A leaf with distinct parts, called leaflets.

Deciduous: Plants that shed their leaves once a year. Mountainous plants are generally winter deciduous, shedding their leaves in winter; desert plants typically shed their leaves in summer (summer deciduous).

Dormancy: When a plant greatly reduces cellular activity.

Drupe: A fleshy fruit with a hard pit inside that contains the seed.

Elliptic: Leaves that are generally symmetrical, narrow and rounded evenly at both ends.

Even-Pinnate Leaf: A leaf in which there are two leaflets joined at the terminating point of a pinnately compound leaf. There is always an even amount of leaflets.

Flower: The reproductive structure of flowering plants (the angiosperms).

Fruit: A mature ovary that contains the seed(s) of the plant.

Herb: A plant used for aromatherapy, cooking, medicine, or seasoning. An herb can be an annual, like chervil, or a tree, like the California bay.

Herbaceous: A plant with few woody stems. Most herbaceous plants are annuals, biennials, or perennials.

Holdfast: The foot that anchors macroalgae, like kelp, to its environment.

Inflorescence: A stem carrying a cluster of flowers.

Lanceolate: A leaf that is lance-like, pointed, narrow, and widest toward the bottom.

Latex: A fluid secretion that is white and gooey.

Leaf: The primary organ for photosynthesis.

Leaflet: A portion of a compound leaf. It generally looks like a leaf, but it is part of a larger ensemble.

Lobed: A division within a leaf that produces a roundish or pointed projection.

Margin: The edges of a leaf. There are many ways to describe leaf margins and this guide tries to stick with lobed, scalloped, serrated, smooth, straight, toothed or wavy.

Midrib: The main vein of a leaf that runs down its center.

Node: The area where leaves and axillary buds attach to a stem.

Obovate: An egg-shaped leaf with the broader portion near the top of the leaf and a rounded or pointed tip.

Odd-Pinnate Leaf: A leaf in which one leaflet is attached at the terminating point of a pinnately compound leaf. There is always an odd amount of leaflets.

Opposite Leaves: Leaves are directly opposite of each other off a central stem, opposed to alternately arranged.

Ovate: An egg-shaped leaf with the wider portion at its base and a rounded or pointed tip.

Palmate: An arrangement that has a central point from which the leaf or leaflets spread out, much like the fingers on a hand.

Palmately Lobed: A leaf that is distinctly divided into 3 or more sections (lobes), much like a fig or a Ribes leaf.

Palmately Compound Leaf: Leaflets that radiate from a central stem, like the California buckeye.

Perennial: A plant that is mostly fleshy and lives longer than two years.

Pesticide: A substance that deters, inhibits or kills a target species, such as a fungus, insect, plant or rodent.

Petal: A colorful and mostly flat appendage of a flower.

Petiole: A small stem that attaches a leaf to a larger stem or stalk.

pH: A measure of acidity and alkalinity. Many species in this guide have pH preferences.

Phototropic: The movement of a plant or leaf in response to light.

Pinnately Lobed: Rounded or pointed protrusions (lobes) found on either side of a central stem; plants with this arrangement include chicory and London rocket.

Pinnately Compound Leaf: A plant with leaflets arranged opposite of each other on a shared stem, as in black walnut. Double compound leaves have multiple stems with leaflets arranged opposite of each other, as in honey locust.

Prostrate: A low-growing plant.

Raceme: An elongated flower stalk with many small stems radiating from it, with each stem bearing flowers.

Rhizome: An underground stem that produces both roots and shoots.

Root: The structure that anchors a plant and absorbs and transports water and nutrients. Most roots are underground, but not all.

Rosette: A group of leaves radiating from a short, stout, central stem, often in a circular fashion.

Seed: A structure that possesses an embryo and stored food.

Seedpod: An enclosure that houses a plant's seeds.

Sepals: The outer parts that enclose a flower.

Serrated Leaves: Leaves with margins that are serrated; the serrations look like tiny teeth.

Shoot: A young stem that can produce leaves.

Simple Leaf: One photosynthesizing structure attached to a stem; these contrast with plants that have leaflets.

Species: A group in which the members shares certain core characteristics and may also be able to interbreed.

Stipe: The stalk or stem of a microalgae (kelp and seaweed).

Stolon: A stem that runs across the top of soil and can produce roots and shoots.

Tendril: A modified leaf used for grasping.

Toothed: A leaf with edges that look like teeth. The edges are deeper and more pronounced than those with serrated edges.

Trifoliate: A leaf consisting of three leaflets, as in black medic, clover, and strawberry.

Umbel: A flower arrangement where the flower stems all join in a central spot, just like the spokes in an umbrella.

Whorl: A ring-like arrangement of leaves on a stem.

Index

ABOUT THE AUTHOR

Douglas Kent MS, MLA

Doug began eating weeds in 1979. His mentor and great aunt, Catherine Peck, was well versed in Depression-Era foods. As a naturalist for the Environmental Nature Center (Newport Beach, CA) in the late 1980s he developed a deep respect for native crafting, eating and living. Since then his love of foraging, gardening and California's landscapes have wildly grown.

Doug has been working in and grazing California's gardens for over 40 years. He has worked on hundreds of landscapes projects throughout the state. He has two advanced degrees in ecological land management. He has volunteered to restoration and urban food efforts in numerous communities. He has taught some aspect of foraging and/or wildcrafting at California State Polytechnic University, Pomona, since 2008. And Doug has written 6 other books on environmental horticulture.

For some people foraging is about survival, to others it is about a spiritual connection with the land. To Doug, foraging is about everyday wellbeing and delight. He believes that California would be far healthier and resilient if we would embrace our nature and graze our impact and weeds.